THE DOMINION OF FAITH

DR. JOE DANIELS

Champions
Publishing
House

THE DOMINION OF FAITH

© 2015 by

DR JOE DANIELS

Published in the United Kingdom by

CHAMPIONS PUBLISHING HOUSE

ISBN 9 780993179105

All rights reserved

No portion of this book may be used without the written permission of the publisher, with the exception of quotes and catchphrases that are designed to imprint the truth shared in the minds and hearts or readers.

For Further Information or permission, please write to:

Champions Publishing House
U6 Gemini Business Park
Leeds. West Yorkshire.

LS7 3JB. UK

Or visit www.fhicc.org for up to date information. All scriptures are from New Kings James Version of the Bible unless otherwise stated.

Table of Contents

Acknowledgements

Introduction...1

Chapter 1 - Background for Faith (Two worlds) 6

Chapter 2 - What is Faith? 27

Chapter 3 - Where and when of Faith 48

Chapter 4 - The Force of Faith? 67

Chapter 5 - Characteristics of Effective Faith 85

Chapter 6 - But - How do I know I'm In Faith? 107

Chapter 7 - The Dominion of faith – Explained 115

Chapter 8 – Faith Boosters – Faith Companions..............142

Chapter 9 - From Faith to Manifestation 160

Notes 166

About The Author 172

Acknowledgments

This book has been inspired by one of the messages once delivered by our father in the faith - the servant of God, Bishop David Oyedepo of Living Faith Worldwide aka Winners Chapel – when he was sharing some important concepts in the definition of faith. I am so grateful for the ministry and tutoring that I and my wife have been receiving from you, Sir. May God continue to exalt your horn, like the horn of a unicorn.

During one of our monthly two-hour mid-week Champions Bible Institute sessions, I expanded and taught on, along these lines with the emphasis on the Force of Faith. Faith being a tangible spiritual force. We intended to have a break between the hours, but I found out that almost 90 minutes into the meeting, almost no-one moved (even including the children). This was a surprise to me. For a mid-week school-term evening service, this was unusual. Somehow, I knew there was an unusual anointing and revelation on this message. The session concluded after two and half hours, with many of the materials that I have presented in this book still to be shared.

While the message was still burning in my spirit, and as I was making an attempt to update and make available my teaching notes, as a hand-out for the session,

I perceived in my spirit that the Holy Spirit would have me make this available in form of an easy to read and easy to complete yet, comprehensive teaching book on the subject of Faith – The God Kind of Faith and its ability to cause us to walk in dominion in life, as God originally intended.

Therefore I wish to acknowledge the undivided attention that I received from my wife, Toyin, and all the FHICC family members that were present during this teaching session. You all helped me to receive the inspiration for this book. I pray that the great revelation on the Concept of the Spiritual Force of Faith - unveiling the tangibility of faith in its workings in the realm of the spirit, will continue to drive us all, in the pursuit of destiny.

To Dr Creflo & Taffi Dollar and Bishop Kenneth & "Mama" Gloria Fuller, of the Creflo Dollar Ministerial Association for coming to our rescue and believing in us and the Vision. You have been a constant source of support and inspiration to us. Bless You Greatly.

My greatest acknowledgement however goes to God and the ministry of the Holy Spirit, who gave me a very intense attention and focus during the preparation of this book. I was present in the body, but not really present, being consumed by an unusual anointing to complete this book.

I am convinced that a Word from the Lord can transform your life permanently for the better, in Jesus Name. As you read this book, do listen to the Voice of the Holy Spirit behind the message of this book. It is your time! I commend this to your spiritual edification and your All-Round Dominion for years to come till eternity.

Dr Joe Daniels

Introduction

The definition of faith is very clearly stated from the scriptures according to Hebrews 11:1 – *"Now Faith is the substance of things hoped for, the evidence of things not seen."* When you look at different translations apart from this King James Version, the definition of faith is somewhat clearer. For example, in the New Century Version, it states: *"Faith means being sure of the things we hope for and knowing that something is real even if we do not see it."*

Or the Amplified Version of Hebrews 11:1 *"Now Faith is the assurance (the confirmation, the title deed) of things [we] hope for, being the proof of things [we] do not see and the conviction of their reality [faith perceiving as real fact what is not revealed to the senses]"*

With a bit of meditation on this scripture verse, the meaning and application becomes even much clearer for many believers. Despite this clarity of the definition, the real life application of faith is still something that many believers - both new and established – find a little challenging. There are real life questions.

What is Faith? How do I apply this faith to my circumstances? How do I know I am really in faith, regarding what I am trusting God for? And this faith "thing" – does it really work, or is it not just positive thinking or being optimistic? Brother so-and-so said, it is because of my lack of faith that I am in this situation, but I really don't think the problem is with me, because I feel I am working by faith. So why is it not working, like "they" said it should?

Many times, the messages from the pulpit and various media do not make it any easier. They often emphasise the importance and the unparalleled benefits that the operation of faith brings. Perhaps even suggesting that, if you can "raise" your faith level, then you will receive manifestation.

Despite this, many believers still wonder, "what position of faith do I really need to take? Why do I need to "think right", "talk right" or match my faith with "corresponding action"? Why can't God just see my sincerity and show me some mercy? Why do I have to walk by faith or "exercise faith, when it's nothing tangible or real?" By design, this is meant to be a collection of "small" books, easy to read, easy to assimilate, yet providing a comprehensive system of truths that is applicable to day to day living.

My trust is that, this book will answer these questions for you and position you squarely in a lifestyle of faith, where the operation of faith is "first nature" to you. My prayer is that, you will have a revelation of the truth that the operations of faith in God or the God-kind of faith is what unleashes you into a life of all-round dominion. Whether spiritual, emotional, physical, mental, academic, professional or materially in the marketplace. Your level of faith will never remain the same, after reading this book. You will receive strength like Sarah, to conceive and deliver your dreams, regardless of how long you have been waiting for your promise or dreams to manifest. Your hour of manifestation has truly come.

The prophetic verdict over your life is that, your spiritual eyes will be opened to see the world of the spirit around you and what is going on in that world, during the periods of your persistent active faith, so that you can continue in patience until manifestation comes.

Likewise, that your spiritual eyes will be opened to see the negative effects of worry, fear, complaining and murmuring - and the damages these attitudes are causing to your glorious destiny - so that you can quickly adjust and re-align your life in the pathway of faith. The next write up below was written in one of our church's weekly e-newsletters. I trust it will also minister to you:

Open Your Faith Account Today

Faith is a Spiritual Force that opens a world of possibilities – that is, faith holds the keys that open impossible doors. Without faith, life will be a struggle. This is because life is full of all sorts of adversities, and faith is your spiritual shield for every flying arrow. (Ephesian 6:16). Faith is also what connects you to God, for the release of His power for your breakthroughs and dominion. Persistent faith keeps you connected until manifestation comes. Faith is important in every vision and dream. A lot of times we give up on God, ourselves, spouse, business, church, profession, friends or family, too quickly, too soon - because of our lack of Faith.

No case is too late for faith. When your faith is at work, your victory in every battle is guaranteed and, time is immaterial.

Can you imagine a life that has no hopes for the future? Or imagine a situation that is impossible? We call this a "hopeless" case. A hopeless life is full of struggles and despair. So without hope, our experience now and in the future will be miserable and depressing.

Faith brings certainty to our hopes and dreams *Faith is the confidence that what we hope for will actually happen; it gives us assurance about things we cannot see. (Hebrews 11:1 NLT)*

Open your faith account today. Start servicing your faith account today, and you will experience some forward motion in destiny. Everyone's result in the pursuit of dream or vision, is a function of the faith at work in them. The Word of God is full of faith-boosting, inspirational events, stories and acts. There is no area of life that is not covered.

As you hear and receive the voice of the Holy Spirit behind the Word of God, faith will settle into your heart by reason of hearing and hearing God's Word. (Romans 10:17)

CHAPTER 1

BACKGROUND FOR FAITH

Two Worlds

The principles of faith in this book are pointers, informing, equipping and instructing you on how to get things done or how to make things happen in your life, by faith.

They are fundamental truths that makes for effective faith that will cause you to have dominion over the affairs of your life. The understanding and working of these principles makes faith work, and enable you to get consistent, not just occasional results. In order to understand faith at all, you must realise that there are two worlds, the physical visible or seen world and the equally tangible but unseen world of the spirit, the invisible unseen realm.

For example, physically, you cannot walk through a wall, but spiritually, you do not have such natural limitations. We contact and interact with the physical world by our five senses but the spiritual world is contacted by faith. In the same way that our eyes, hands, ears, nose and tongue can appreciate what is going on around us, similarly, our faith and spiritual perception can appreciate what is going on in the spirit realm.

There is no doubt that there is an unseen tangible realm or spiritual dimension. The unseen realm is governed by certain spiritual laws in the same way that the physical world is governed by certain physical laws. The laws of faith are some of these spiritual laws. The laws of faith are similar to the laws of gravity. They will work for whosoever works or engages with it.

That is why the laws of faith works for non-believers, just like it does for believers. Gravity is universal, in the same way that faith is universal. Non-believers though, cannot have the God-kind of Faith, until they have received the nature of God, by accepting Jesus Christ, as the Lord and Saviour of their lives.

The truth is that, spiritual operations can affect and change natural or physical operations. That is, the spiritual world can and does affect the natural physical world, both for good and for bad. However, the world of the spirit is more powerful than the physical world because, many of the restrictions of time, space, place or person do not occur in the spirit realm.

Spiritual power is much stronger than physical power. It is possible to release the force of faith regarding a matter, in London; yet see its effect in New York or Hong Kong or anywhere that the force of faith is directed.

God of Eternal NOW

To understand the realm of the spirit, you must understand that God dwells in an eternal timelessness - called **NOW**. He is Alpha and Omega, the Beginning and the End. This means that in His realm, beginning and the end exit together, such that time, in terms of chronology according to human physical experience does not matter to Him. What matters more is set time, in terms of when all things are ready or in place.

So also, if we must receive from God and make things happen by faith, we must understand this concept. **It is always NOW with God**, that is why He is the same yesterday, today and forever. When you pray, in His realm, He answers **NOW.**

When you pray according to His Word, (Mark 11:24), there is no "time" in His realm of existence. How you relate to time in the physical world though, is different because, you can observe night and day, days to weeks, weeks to months and months to years. With God however, in the realm of the spirit, it's always **NOW**.

He is Jehovah and dwells in light, Heaven is His throne and the earth is His footstool. So one of the lessons of faith, is to learn, how to reach into timelessness, of the realm of the Spirit and bring it into time and place, in the natural realm.

"And he said unto me, O Daniel, a man greatly beloved, understand the words that I speak unto thee, and stand upright: for unto thee am I now sent. And when he had spoken this word unto me, I stood trembling. Then said he unto me, fear not, Daniel: for from the first day that thou didst set thine heart to understand, and to chasten thyself before thy God, thy words were heard, and I am come for thy words.

But the prince of the kingdom of Persia withstood me one and twenty days: but, lo, Michael, one of the chief princes, came to help me; and I remained there with the kings of Persia. Now I am come to make thee understand what shall befall thy people in the latter days: for yet the vision is for many days." (Daniel 10:11-14 KJV)

So, in these scripture verses, we can see two things here, as we see similarly in Daniel 9:23: that, as soon as Daniel's entreaty and prayer reached heaven, the answer was dispatched. It also gives us an idea of what was happening in the realm of the spirit, that there was a "prince", a territorial spiritual entity over the kingdom of Persia, and this entity withstood Daniel's angel for twenty-one days (according to time in the natural realm), until in the spirit realm, a Divine reinforcement came through Angel Michael. It was only then that, Daniel's angel could be allowed to deliver his message to him.

There is certainly a world of the spirit, which is very tangible and real, in addition to the world that we can see. **The fact that you cannot physically see something, does not mean that, it does not exist.** There is the physical eyes and there is the spiritual eyes.

"While we look not at the things which are seen, but at the things which are not seen: for the things which are seen are temporal; but the things which are not seen are eternal." (2 Corinthians 4:18)

So it is possible to "look" out and see the things that cannot be seen with the physical eyes, by using our spiritual eyes. Here it says that, the things that, cannot be seen are more lasting; they are eternal, while the physical, visible things are temporary.

On this understanding of the two worlds, we can see that, things exist in the spirit realm. When these things are made visible in the physical realm, we call it "manifestation" - the appearing or display or showing of what existed before, but was hidden or was not yet visible - but later became visible. **The time of manifestation is not when those things first exist. This is when they become manifested in the physical sense.** This is very important.

For example, the ability for Man to be able to sit in a comfortable leather chair was first conceived in the unseen realm. To the person(s) who conceived it, it was very real. It is following that conception that efforts, knowledge, skills, ideas and determination then go into the process of making it (manifestation). The leather chair has "existed" before it became manifest. With God, and with us, as children of God, similar things do happen.

This is a reality that is applicable to whatever can be conceived. The time of existence, is the time it is conceived, whether by thoughts, imaginations, heart desires or words. The process of time – which is **NOW** with God – is what it takes for that which existed in the unseen realm, to become manifest in the visible realm. Now, when you imagine that God's supernatural power and unseen agents – like Angels - become involved in the process, you can see how the position of faith can cause some mind-boggling things – miracles – to take place. You are next in line for a miracle, by the operation of your Faith in God.

Two Kinds of Faith

To take this further, in the same way that there are two worlds – the physical and the spiritual, there are two kinds of faith –

1. Sense –Knowledge based Faith and
2. Revelation-knowledge based Faith

Sense-knowledge based faith is founded, centred and established on the five senses. It's believe system is based on what is materially tangible - that can be seen, touched, explained, heard, tasted, smelt, handled or experienced.

This faith is based on the evidence that can be or has been proven. For example doctors can cure many infections, so someone with sense-knowledge faith believes that when he/she goes to the doctor to get antibiotics, he/she will get better. Similarly, someone with sense knowledge faith believes that if he/she has been interviewed for a job, and has been offered the job, then that job indeed exists.

Sense-knowledge faith causes the person to start preparing and making necessary arrangement, such as child care or buying new clothes (sometimes with borrowed money), in order to start this job.

This person starts work, and spends money daily in relation to this work, including transport costs, until he/she gets the first pay either one, two or four weeks later. The expectation is that they are going to get a salary at the due date. He/she has demonstrated sense-knowledge faith, based on experience and what is physically visible. Thomas only believed what made sense and what he could see, about the resurrection of Jesus – this is sense-knowledge "faith".

"But Thomas, one of the twelve, called Didymus, was not with them when Jesus came. The other disciples therefore said unto him, we have seen the LORD. But he said unto them, except I shall see in his hands the print of the nails, and put

my finger into the print of the nails, and thrust my hand into his side, I will not believe." (John 20:24-25 KJV)

However, do take note of the comments that Jesus made in the following verses, in response to Thomas' position:

"And after eight days His disciples were again inside, and Thomas with them. Jesus came, the doors being shut, and stood in the midst, and said, "Peace to you!" Then He said to Thomas, "Reach your finger here, and look at my hands; and reach your hand here, and put it into my side. Do not be unbelieving, but believing." (John 20: 26-27)

Jesus rebuked Thomas for not believing, what he couldn't see. Jesus declared a blessing – a spiritual advantage or empowerment – on those who have not seen, yet believed. This is the foundation of the Christian Faith.

"And Thomas answered and said to Him, "My Lord and my God!" Jesus said to him, "Thomas, because you have seen me, you have believed. Blessed are those who have not seen and yet have believed." (John 20:28-29)

The apostle Paul, also emphasised the importance of not living in the sense-knowledge realm, rather, to become aware of the fact that our Christian Faith rests on believing in what cannot be seen.

"Whom having not seen you love. Though now you do not see Him, yet believing, you rejoice with joy inexpressible and

full of glory, receiving the end of your faith—the salvation of your souls." (1Peter 1:8-9)

In conclusion, sense knowledge based faith is determined by what is tangible – that is, what is noticeable, concrete, touchable and real to the senses. Revelation-knowledge based faith however, is the opposite. It relies on what is not necessarily physically tangible. However, just because something is not immediately physically tangible, does not mean it is not real. The issue is the reality of the person, who is trying to perceive.

Moving From Sense-Knowledge Faith

You must understand that sense-knowledge based faith is limited in what it can do or make possible. It is therefore, important for the believer in Christ to move on from operating in sense-knowledge to operating in the revelation-knowledge based faith.

"Jesus said to him, "Thomas, because you have seen me, you have believed. Blessed are those who have not seen and yet have believed." (John 20:29)

Learning to believe and operate in that which cannot be seen does take time and spiritual discipline, as we will see later in this book. However, it is the operation of this kind and level of faith that will usher the believer into the realm of spiritual dominion.

When you consider the fact that we are moment by moment, constantly being bombarded with information and reports, which are not necessarily in alignment with the realities of God's kind of faith, it is even more important that we guard our hearts, to avoid being negatively programmed for failure, mishaps and spiritual bondages in life.

Faith in God and operation by the faith of God is a foundational principle for every believer. **It is a subject that must be mastered, in order to become a master over the circumstances of life and living.** Your victory is here already!

Revelation-Knowledge Based Faith

Revelation-knowledge based Faith is also based on what is tangible – that is, what is noticeable, concrete, touchable and real. The difference is that, it is what is *spiritually* tangible, concrete, touchable and real, that formed the basis of revelation-knowledge based faith.

Revelation (*Greek word apokalupsis*) means an unveiling, a disclosure or making visible of things which before then was not visible. A great example of revelation is what happened when the king sent a warrant of arrest for Prophet Elisha, who was on the mountain, following a false accusation of being involved in a conspiracy designed to undermine the king's military defence.

The servant of the prophet was afraid, as he felt quite helpless. The prophet reassured him on the basis of his revelation and let the servant in on the reality of the invisible, yet tangible realm of Divine Security and Divine Protection:

*"And he answered, fear not: for they that be with us are more than they that be with them. And Elisha prayed, and said, L*ORD*, I pray thee, open his eyes, that he may see. And the L*ORD* opened the eyes of the young man; and he saw: and, behold, the mountain was full of horses and chariots of fire round about Elisha." (2 Kings 6:16-17)*

Another example is when Peter received revelation that Jesus is the Christ – the Messiah. Jesus said that Peter's answer was based on revealed knowledge, not from what he knew by himself.

"And Simon Peter answered and said, Thou art the Christ, the Son of the living God. And Jesus answered and said unto him, Blessed art thou, Simon Barjona: for flesh and blood hath not revealed it unto thee, but my Father which is in heaven." (Matthew 16:16-17)

When our faith is based on this kind of revelation knowledge, it is called revelation-knowledge based faith. Of course there are various degrees of revelations, so also there are various degrees of faith. When faith is based on this kind of revelation, it is difficult to doubt the existence of that which one has seen in the realm of the spirit or by unusual inner conviction of reality.

We can therefore conclude that spiritual things can be seen, and can be just as real, as physical things. It takes the operation of the Holy Spirit to imprint this into one's heart. This is the beginning of faith! *Faith begins when the revealed truth of God's Word, concerning a matter is known*.

Truth versus Facts

Revelation here is also based on the truth. The truth is exactly the way it is. Facts are based on what is generally known based on the information given. So when faith is based on the facts, it is sense-knowledge based faith and when it is based on revealed truth, it is revelation-knowledge based faith.

For example, if I installed a Ferrari engine in the body of a Toyota car. The truth is that, the Toyota is indeed a Ferrari, because it is the Ferrari engine that drives it. The fact is that, anyone that sees the Toyota body will call it a Toyota car (that's the fact), and unless they know (because someone revealed to them what has been done), they will even argue that it's a Toyota car - in essence, though, it is a Ferrari car. The fact on the basis of what can be seen is that, the car is a Toyota, but the truth is that, the car is indeed a Ferrari, as that is the engine that drives it.

Now **the Word of God is the Truth**, and it cannot be changed, no matter what the visible appearance might be; regardless of what the facts may be, it does not change the Truth. The truth is not dependent on opinion, culture, nationality, education or gender. Truth is constant, and therefore reliable. Accepting the Truth of the Word of God, that has been revealed is the beginning of revelation-knowledge based faith. It is the key to experiencing the supernatural of God's Kingdom.

"For My thoughts are not your thoughts, nor are your ways my ways," says the LORD. For as the heavens are higher than the earth, so are my ways higher than your ways, and my thoughts than your thoughts. For as the rain comes down, and the snow from heaven, And do not return there, But water the earth, And make it bring forth and bud, That it may give seed to the sower And bread to the eater, So shall My word be that goes forth from My mouth; It shall not return to Me void, But it shall accomplish what I please, And it shall prosper in the thing for which I sent it." (Isaiah 55: 8-11)

Faith Should Be the Believers Way of Life

It is difficult to have a meaningful Christian walk without the exercise of faith in one way, form or another. Several scriptures state the reason why the walk of faith is crucial to the believer's day to day living. For a start, we walk or live by faith, not by what we see.

"For we walk by faith, not by sight" (2 Corinthians 5:7)

We are made to have a right-standing with God, by faith, and we continue to position our lifestyle in righteousness by faith. We cannot boast of our good works, because we can only be considered righteous, by trusting in the finished work of Christ.

"But that no man is justified by the law in the sight of God, it is evident: for, the just shall live by faith." (Galatians 3:11)

"For therein is the righteousness of God revealed from faith to faith: as it is written, the just shall live by faith" (Romans 1:17)

"Behold, his soul which is lifted up is not upright in him: but the just shall live by his faith". (Habakkuk 2:4)

We categorically cannot please God, except by faith. God derives no pleasure in the life of someone who refuses to walk by faith towards Him.

"Now the just shall live by faith: but if any man draw back, my soul shall have no pleasure in him" (Hebrews 10:38)

Although it is impossible to please God without faith, walking by faith commits God to work on our behalf. It commits God and releases His power for us to walk in dominion and to rule in the world of possibilities.

"But without faith it is impossible to please him: for he that cometh to God must believe that he is, and that he is a rewarder of them that diligently seek him" (Hebrews 11:6)

Also, it is difficult to get answers to prayers, without faith. It is impossible, when it comes to asking God for wisdom, but it also applies to other areas. The operation of faith is a basic spiritual law of asking or a prayer of petition, where we ask God for what our hearts desire. (See also - Mark 11:24)

"If any of you lack wisdom, let him ask of God, that giveth to all men liberally, and upbraideth not; and it shall be given him. But let him ask in faith, nothing wavering.

For he that wavereth is like a wave of the sea driven with the wind and tossed. For let not that man think that he shall receive any thing of the Lord. A double minded man is unstable in all his ways." (James 1:5-8)

The New Century Version says, God is, *"generous to everyone and will give you wisdom without criticizing you"* when you ask.

It also adds *"But when you ask God, you must believe and not doubt...Such doubters are thinking two different things at the same time, they should not think they will receive anything...."*

We Subdue Kingdoms by Faith

There is yet another very important reason why we must learn and become established in the operation of faith. It is through faith that we subdue kingdoms. To "subdue" means to bring under: to conquer by force or exert a superior power over, and bring into permanent subjection. It means to reduce, calm or pacify, under dominion. To subdue implies that one overpowers so as to disable from further resistance. It means to crush, to destroy the force of, or render submissive, or bring under the command of.

So faith causes us to walk in unquestionable dominion and authority and superiority over "kingdoms". Kingdoms refer to authorities, sovereign powers, or territory or country subject to the rule of a king or queen. Kingdom is a domain, in which something is dominant or where something or someone is in charge. It could mean a particular environment or walk of life, or even a bad habit or failing business.

Therefore, to subdue kingdoms by faith, means to use the principles and laws of faith that we are going to learn in this book, as revealed in the Bible, to dominate over all the three areas of human living, and over the affairs of life, community, and nations.

It means to be in command and authority (under God), over what happens, in one's spirit, soul and body, as it relates to one's home, relationships, business, family, ministry, profession and anything else one is engaged in. Look at the rest of the verses in Hebrews Chapter 11

"Who through faith subdued kingdoms, wrought righteousness, obtained promises, stopped the mouths of lions, quenched the violence of fire, escaped the edge of the sword, out of weakness were made strong, waxed valiant in fight, turned to flight the armies of the aliens. Women received their dead raised to life again: and others were tortured, not accepting deliverance; that they might obtain a better resurrection" (Hebrews 11:33-35)

So, it is by faith that we live and do right. It is by faith we obtain promises. We stop all oppositions, be it spiritual, emotional, physical or natural. Every violence or attack or sword against us is crushed and brought under control. They are conquered and brought into permanent subjection, by the force and power of faith.

We will learn shortly that faith is a tangible spiritual force, dynamic in its working, and able to release the power of God on our behalf, and at the same time, being double-edged, it is able to overpower, terminate, disable and subdue the operations of darkness. The devil has been defeated.

We Are Strengthened By Faith

Lastly, we find from the above scripture that we are strengthened by faith, in the midst of things what should naturally make us weak. The strength and courage that flows from the operations of faith is undeniable.

We fight on valiantly, in the battle of life and turn to flight the armies of the aliens or strangers to the Covenant. Whatever should be alive in your lives that is dead, becomes resurrected back to life, by the power of faith. No wonder the bible says:

"For whatever is born of God overcomes the world. And this is the victory that has overcome the world—our faith. Who is he who overcomes the world, but he who believes that Jesus is the Son of God?" (1 John 5:4-5).

Contend Earnestly For the Faith

I hope it is now easy for you to understand the reason why the bible instructs us to contend for this overcoming faith, seeing so much that can be achieved and the beauty and colour it can bring to the life of a believer.

"Beloved, when I gave all diligence to write unto you of the common salvation, it was needful for me to write unto you, and exhort you that ye should earnestly contend for the faith which was once delivered unto the saints" (Jude 1:3)

To earnestly contend for the faith means to fight vigorously to keep our faith alive and strong in God! It's like saying, whatever you do in life, make sure your faith does not falter; defend it at all cost! Don't let go of your faith. The enemy or even just circumstances in life will put pressure on your faith.

"Fight the good fight of faith, lay hold on eternal life, whereunto thou art also called, and hast professed a good profession before many witnesses" (1 Timothy 6:12)

"Jesus said, in the world, you shall have tribulation, but be of good cheer, because I have overcome the world" (John16:33).

Jesus also tells the story of the two men in Matthew 7:24-33 – one built his house on the rock and the adversities of life came, like the flood, rain and winds but the house stood, because of its solid foundation. The other one was built upon sand, and when the same pressures came upon him, the house collapsed in a mighty way.

So we can conclude that, it is not so much the floods, winds, rains, problems or crises of life that defeats a man. It is the fact that, the man does or does not have the necessary victorious life foundations that determines the outcomes of every life battle engagement. So, **life happens,** and it is what you are made of, physically, emotionally and spiritually, that determines your coping strategies or ability to withstand all life's pressure. The solid foundation here is being a **"hearer"** and a **"doer"** of the Word of God. It is very crucial in contending for our faith. I declare over your life, that your faith will not fail.

"So, *be sober, be vigilant; because your adversary the devil, as a roaring lion, walketh about, seeking whom he may devour: Whom resist steadfast in the faith, knowing that the same afflictions are accomplished in your brethren that are in the world. But the God of all grace, who hath called us unto his eternal glory by Christ Jesus, after that ye have suffered a while, make you perfect, stablish, strengthen, settle you"* (1 Peter 5:8-10)

Regardless of what the enemy does, to try to devour you or devour your faith, as you remain vigilant and **RESIST STEADFAST IN THE FAITH**, you will see victory in Jesus Name. The scriptures also reminds us that this is a common thing, that the enemy seeks to devour us, but God turns it around to our advantage.

God uses the same situations to mature, establish, strengthen and settle us. Again we see that even on the adversities of life, it is not God's Will for us to be defeated, but to overcome.

There is no temptation or trials that may come our way, that God has not made a way of escape and the strength to bear, for us, which spiritual deposit or virtue of strength, courage and stability are being established in us.

"No temptation has overtaken you except such as is common to man; but God is faithful, who will not allow you to be tempted beyond what you are able, but with the temptation will also make the way of escape, that you may be able to bear it" (1 Corinthians 10:13)

The Apostle James encourages us in his inspired letter:

"My brethren, count it all joy when you fall into various trials, ³ knowing that the testing of your faith produces patience. ⁴ But let patience have its perfect work, that you may be perfect and complete, lacking nothing" (James 1:2-4)

In conclusion, it is important to note that **YOUR FAITH IS WORTH FIGHTING FOR.** It is what opens you up to the world of dominion, as you exercise your power and authority in Christ Jesus, by faith.

CHAPTER 2

WHAT IS FAITH?

"Now faith is the substance of things hoped for, the evidence of things not seen" (Hebrews 11:1)

"Now faith is confidence in what we hope for and assurance about what we do not see" (Hebrews 11:1 NIV) and (Hebrews 11:1, AMP):

"NOW FAITH is the assurance (the confirmation, the title deed) of the things [we] hope for, being the proof of things [we] do not see and the conviction of their reality [faith perceiving as real fact what is not revealed to the senses]"

Practical Functional Definition of Faith

I was privileged to attend a conference during which Bishop David Oyedepo, our Father in the Lord, gave a series of insight on what faith is, using the various scriptural events in the Bible where men or women of God achieved so much by faith.

The book of Hebrews mentioned many of those men and women in the "hall of fame" of faith. I trust that these series of practical definitions of faith will bring what faith is, to your consciousness and understanding as God reveals to you, what your responsibilities are in the journey of faith. I have adapted some of the definitions, in order to help clarify the thought process of readers, in a way that I trust God will make it directly applicable to you, in the NOW.

What Is Faith?

1. Faith is the Spiritual Medium through which we tap into the power of the Almighty God.

It's the channel that connects us to the flow of the Power of God for a change of situation. It helps us to tap into virtue for our desired change. In other words, if you consider what James 1:5-8 requires us to do when it comes to asking for wisdom, (we must ask in faith), it is reasonable based on scriptures to say that Faith is a supernatural avenue or medium, through which we can tap into the Power of God, when we need it. So if you need the power of God in your life, you know you can have it, and you know how you can tap into it, through the operation of faith. Faith is not a natural visible virtue, it is a spiritual virtue.

We see several examples in the Bible, where people tapped into the Power of God, and the power was released to help address their issues. Faith is what connects them. **Faith Is The Connector**. Faith is like the plug you put into the electrical socket. Electricity is flowing. You cannot see it. Let's say, there is an electrical equipment like a television. That television will not work and cannot access the electrical power, unless it is connected. **Faith is the plug** and the cable wire that connects to the power to drive the required outcome.

Let's use the analogy of the power socket and the television. Bartimaeus was in a position of need for healing of his blind eyes. He, or rather his body, or his blind eyes, are like the television. Jesus represented power, the electric power - the anointing flowing through him – necessary to power and open Bartimaeus' blind eyes.

When Bartimaeus heard about Jesus passing by, something was injected into him, which concluded that Jesus could help him have his eyesight back. It was that something, that made him to start shouting for mercy. That something empowered him, not to be shouted down by the disciples. That "something", springing from the hope of healing, is called Faith. That's why Jesus made the comment in this concluding phase of the miracles.

"Then Jesus said to him, "Go your way; your faith has made you well." And immediately he received his sight and followed Jesus on the road" (Mark 10:52)

Jesus said Bartimaeus' faith has healed him of his blindness. What Jesus is saying here, is that, it was Bartimaeus' faith that connected to the power that was available to heal. Bartimaeus' faith is like the plug and the wire, which connected to the power source. It drew out the power from the Anointing Junction.

Faith is the spiritual medium through which we tap into the power of the Almighty God. It's the channel that connects us to the flow of the power of God for a change of situation. It helps us to tap into the virtue for our desired change.

2. Faith is not just believing God, it is obeying God to prove that you believe Him, so as to commit Him to make good His promises. "Faith is obeying" or "Faith is doing" based on what God has said in His Word

Please understand that, faith is the believing and acting on what one believes, "faith" and "believe" are not the same. It is possible to believe and not act on what one believes. Faith is not faith, without corresponding action. So if God in His Mightiness says something, and we believe Him, or if He gives an instruction and we believe that instruction (His Word), and then ignore His instruction or set aside His views, it is just the same as not believing Him. Remember that:

"Without faith, it is impossible to please God." (Hebrews 11:6)

God is therefore not satisfied with the person who does not trust Him enough to make good His Word. He is not satisfied with the person who refuses to act on or obey His instructions. It is like making God a liar or unreliable. That is why the children of Israel were always getting on the wrong side of God. How can two work together, except they are in agreement? (Amos 3:3).

Our obedience to His instruction is an expression of agreement with Him. When what He tells us is not easily understood, or doesn't make sense, but we believe Him anyway, and act in recognition of Him as the Almighty God, then that is faith. Let's look at some examples, in the following passages, which are the summaries of historical event which occurred in the Old Testament:

"By faith Noah, being divinely warned of things not yet seen, moved with godly fear, prepared an ark for the saving of his household, by which he condemned the world and became heir of the righteousness which is according to faith. By faith Abraham obeyed when he was called to go out to the place which he would receive as an inheritance. And he went out, not knowing where he was going" (Hebrews 11:7-8)

Although there has been no recorded history of rain, up to this time in history, and therefore, Noah did not understand what God was saying per se, he believed God and acted in line with his believe. And although, to Noah, what God instructed him to do did not make sense, to him, as a limited man, He believed in the Almighty God, as the final authority. He simply acted.

Similarly, Abraham did not know where God was asking Him to go and what the challenges were likely to be. He simply obeyed God's Word and left his home country to the land of the unknown.

These two men, and many others in scriptures, simply committed God to making good His Word, by obeying what He commanded. This is Faith in the Invisible and Invincible God.

Faith is not just believing God, it is obeying God to prove that you believe Him, so as to commit Him to make good His promises. Faith Is Obeying or Doing - based on what God has said in His Word. They obeyed and acted, on the basis of what God had said.

Let's look at James 2:14-26. These twelve verses by the Apostle help to clarify the truth that **"Faith is not Faith, unless there is corresponding action to it"**. Faith acts. If there is no action, then it is not faith.

"Thus also faith by itself, if it does not have works, is dead. But someone will say, "You have faith, and I have works." Show me your faith without your works, and I will show you my faith by my works. You believe that there is one God. You do well. Even the demons believe—and tremble! But do you want to know, O foolish man, that faith without works is dead? Was not Abraham our father justified by works when

he offered Isaac his son on the altar? Do you see that faith was working together with his works, and by works faith was made perfect? And the Scripture was fulfilled which says, "Abraham believed God, and it was accounted to him for righteousness."

And he was called the friend of God. You see then that a man is justified by works, and not by faith only. Likewise, was not Rahab the harlot also justified by works when she received the messengers and sent them out another way? For as the body without the spirit is dead, so faith without works is dead also." (James 2:14-26).

It is not possible to be alive in the body, if the spirit has left the body. Similarly, it is not possible to have faith, if works or action is not simultaneously present.

Another way of saying this is that, **Faith is Works, based on and backed by believe in God's Word. It is putting Gods word to work, so as to commit His integrity to perform whatever He tells you to do - causing signs to follow your life**.

God's Word is applicable to every area of life. God's Word Is Seed (Mark 4). The Word of God, like the Seed, has got no other destiny but to produce fruit. When we find a scripture that addresses an issue in our life, it is like finding a seed. To produce, it must fall on good ground and it must survive every attack of deception and affliction, which makes us doubt the Word. Then it must survive the cares of life and deceit of other non-Word based alternatives. And it must be cultivated in a good ground to bring forth multiple fields of harvest.

This process takes varying times and it also depends on what it is being applied to. Faith does what is required to be done. It puts that seed to the ground, applies the Word to the situation in faith, and doing whatever the Word instructs. This action, especially when it is taken in the face of contrary evidence is faith.

"His mother saith unto the servants, whatsoever he saith unto you, do it." (John 2:5). "Jesus saith unto them, Fill the waterpots with water. And they filled them up to the brim." And he saith unto them, Draw out now, and bear unto the governor of the feast. And they bare it" (John 2:7-8, KJV)

The servants put Jesus' Word to work, based on encouragement from Jesus' mother. Although what Jesus instructed them to do did not make sense, it was this action or obedience in faith that committed the power of God to flow in the miracle of turning water into wine at the wedding party in Galilee. The experience of Peter serves to explain this further:

"Now when he had left speaking, he said unto Simon, lunch out into the deep, and let down your nets for a draught" And Simon answering said unto him, Master, we have toiled all the night, and have taken nothing: nevertheless at thy word I will let down the net" And they beckoned unto their partners,

which were in the other ship, that they should come and help them. And they came, and filled both the ships, so that they began to sink" (Luke 5:4-6)

Peter here acknowledges his willingness to trust and exercise faith, despite his natural mind or senses telling him otherwise. He stated his position, such as "this is not what I will do ordinarily, because it doesn't make sense. I have too much expertise to believe that what you are telling me is not a waste of time. However, I also want to exercise faith; and even though my mind is telling me this is stupid, nevertheless at thy word – because you asked me to, I will do what you said". This is faith.

This ability to put the Word to work in this way, is faith. It commits the anointing of Jesus, to deliver a financial miracle and business turnaround for Peter and his business partner.

3. Faith is the unflinching, unreserved display of confidence in God until the desired result is obtained.

"Cast not away therefore your confidence, which hath great recompense of reward. For ye have need of patience, that, after ye have done the will of God, ye might receive the promise. For yet a little while, and he that shall come will come, and will not tarry. Now the just shall live by faith: but if any man draw back, my soul shall have no pleasure in him" (Hebrews 10:35-38 KJV)

Confidence is assurance and trust. Confidence however, is not the same as faith. It is possible to have assurance in the ability of a doctor or medication to heal a certain disease. However, if after taking this medication or being given the conventional treatment, cure or result is not forth coming, it is natural to lose confidence - either in the doctor or the medication. Faith, however, is unwavering, undaunted, resolute and persistent assurance that the healing is possible, despite what the evidence or the doctor says.

Faith taps into the realm of the spirit, where the answer has been received, based on the Word and prayer. Faith knows that the healing exists - in not-yet-tangible form - so there is assurance. Faith then goes beyond this; it stands in this position, doing whatever it takes, until the desired result or healing takes place. That is why we are encouraged here in Hebrews 10:35, not to throw away our confidence, because delay is not denial and the just shall live by standing in that position of assurance, until "he that will come, will come and will not delay."

This ability not to waver until there is manifestation is called patience. So you can almost say that faith is confidence, plus works, plus patience, lasting till the result is obtained. Alternatively, we can say that faith is confidently unwaveringly working and walking in obedience and patience, until the desired outcome is obtained.

On the basis of this, we see that, Faith endures the period when it looks like nothing is working, when the prevailing circumstances seems contrary to that which is ultimately expected. This leads us to the other practical definition of faith.

4. Faith is being fully persuaded of the Truth, the prevailing circumstances notwithstanding, until there is manifestation.

The truth is unchangeable and real. It cannot be improved or altered. So faith is based on the Truth. Whatever God says is the Truth. God's Word is the Truth. When faith is based primarily on the Word of God, the foundation for that faith is eternal and reliable. It is a sure foundation. Faith that is based on eternal Word must be eternal. Can you see with your spiritual eyes?

Faith that is tagged to the Word will keep going until that Word ceases, and the Word of God cannot cease. Jesus said that heaven and earth shall pass away, but not a jot of the Word of God will pass away. **In other words, faith has the capacity to outlast and triumph over the circumstances for which faith is being applied.**

Remember that, circumstances are usually never permanent. Circumstances are dynamic; being temporary, they are subject to change. The Word of God though, is not subject to change. Whatever God says is final. He has the final verdict. Anything else is temporary. We see this at work, in the life of Abraham. God had already spoken the Word of promise, according to Genesis 17: 4-5.

"As for me, behold, my covenant is with you, and you shall be a father of many nations.[5] No longer shall your name be called Abram, but your name shall be Abraham; for I have made you a father of many nations"

This Word is the Truth. *"….I have made thee a father of many nations".* As far as God was concerned He had already conferred on Abraham, what it takes and has already made him the father of many nations. In other words, Abraham was already a father of many nations, even when he and Sarah had not yet produced and given birth to Isaac. He said, *"As for me …."*

In speaking the Truth, God does not refer to the natural or the visible or earthly timing for saying what He has said. Remember God dwells in an eternal NOW, and there is no time limit with God. That's why He could say, "I have MADE thee." As far as God is concerned Abraham had already been made a Father of many nations, even though his prevailing circumstances had not changed. So this quality of God, to speak from His realm of dwelling, is brought into focus in the passage. That, God speaks of those things that be not (to the visible realm), as if they were.

God talks often in past tense, concerning His promises because they are settled and are as good as already done. It is meant to reassure us, about the faithfulness and commitment of God to see that His Word comes to past in our lives. **When we also walk in this spirit of faith, we will speak of those things that do not exist, as though they already existed. Faith is speaking the future now, in the present, as if it is already past.** The God kind of faith transcends time, in the same way that God transcends time.

"As it is written, I have made thee a father of many nations,) before him whom he believed, even God, who quickeneth the dead, and calleth those things which be not as though they were" (Romans 4:17)

Having this understanding about the spirituality of faith, we can then understand this definition and explain the actions of Abraham's position in faith. Faith is being fully persuaded of the Truth, the prevailing circumstances notwithstanding, until there is manifestation.

"Who against hope believed in hope, that he might become the father of many nations; according to that which was spoken, so shall thy seed be".

The prevailing circumstance in the life of Abraham was that, he did not have a child of his own with Sarah, his wife. The prevailing circumstance was that – it was already past the usual reproductive age, for both of them, especially for Sarah. The prevailing circumstance was that, their situation was naturally impossible, there was no solution. Nothing and nobody could help them. All hope was gone.

However, God's promises remained. God remained committed to His Word. God did not change His mind about Abraham. The promises still stood. Abraham had to make a conscious decision to either believe the promises of God despite the prevailing circumstances or believe the circumstances.

If he believed the circumstances, there was no hope. If he believed God, then there was still hope – the prevailing circumstances notwithstanding. So against the hopeless situation, Abraham hoped in the Word. That is faith. This faith however, must remain steadfast, till manifestation comes. With further delayed manifestation, it is possible for faith to become weak. So in order for faith not to become weak, what did Abraham do?

"And being not weak in faith, he considered not his own body now dead, when he was about an hundred years old, neither yet the deadness of Sarah's womb. He staggered not at the promise of God through unbelief; but was strong in faith, giving glory to God. And being fully persuaded that, what he had promised, he was able also to perform." (Romans 4:19-21)

There are three things that Abraham did, so that his faith would not become weak or burn out; three things that will enhance the persistence of faith, during the period of patience, when manifestation is on its way. When we look at the force of faith, you will understand that from beginning of faith to manifestation, the process should not stop.

There is something going on behind the scene, in the spirit realm, that is strategizing to work together, to ensure that the manifestation of the promises is good, regardless of the time it takes. This is where the Wisdom of God comes into play. If only God can open your eyes, to see what is happening when we persist in faith, you will not back down because of delayed manifestation. The process only comes to a halt, when we give up, or lose our confidence. Now, let's look at those three things that Abraham did:

First, (v. 19) – Abraham refused to consider the natural evidence against him. He did not focus on or put emphasis on the physical circumstances, but on the truth, that God who had promised cannot lie. That, there was no way, His promises was not going to become manifest. At this stage, he had come to the point where he received his son by faith in the spirit realm. It took him some time to get to this place of absolute faith, but once he got there, nothing was going to shift him, from expecting otherwise.

Secondly, (v. 20) – Abraham did not stagger at the promise of God, through unbelief, once he came to that place of faith. Unbelief causes us to stagger or waver or become unsettled regarding the promises of God. Abraham did not stagger. In the chapters ahead, we will look at how to know you are in faith.

Suffice to say, that if you are staggering, you are not in faith. To stagger means to doubt, or hesitate, but in the original use of the Greek word - *diakrino* – it means to separate oneself in a hostile spirit, to oppose, strive with dispute or contend. It means to be at variance with oneself.

So to stagger in this sense connotes a lot of inner turbulence, inner arguments or oppositions about whether the promise is going to come to pass or not, or doubting whether the word of God is true or not. It can also be extended to mean, inner contentions or strife or disappointment or hostility towards the experience or journey of faith. When there is no staggering, strong faith persists. Strong faith will give glory to God, even in the face of delays, rather than mourn or complain or worry. We will talk more about this later.

The third thing that Abraham did, that helped him to have persistence of faith, was to come to a place of complete trust in God. He considered the greatness of God and His ability and willingness to do what He promised. He came to conclude in full persuasion that God cannot lie – if He has promised, He will make good His promise.

That is a place of rest. He was not troubled by his circumstances; he was actively engaging God in praise. It is important to note that this is not a place of passive waiting. It is a place of active engagement in another force of the spirit, which is to provoke God to action, and at the same time to force out any obstacles to the manifestation.

This is what praise does. **Praise is double-edged, just as faith**. On one hand, it provokes God to action, and on the other hand, it strikes at the heart of every opposition of darkness or any other opposing force(s), and flushes out every hindrance(s) and lay claim of that which God has promised.

Reminder: Faith is being fully persuaded of the Truth, the prevailing circumstances notwithstanding, until there is manifestation. The word of God is designed to continue to be operative, until, it prospers the one who puts it to work.

"For as the rain cometh down, and the snow from heaven, and returneth not thither, but watereth the earth, and maketh it bring forth and bud, that it may give seed to the sower, and bread to the eater:

So shall my word be that goeth forth out of my mouth: it shall not return unto me void, but it shall accomplish that which I please, and it shall prosper in the thing whereto I sent it." (Isaiah 55:8-11)

Faith Partnership and Responsibility:

Faith Is Not Will-Power

Faith is not passive or one sided. In the operation of faith, it is important to understand that faith is not Will-Power. It is impossible to operate in the God Kind of Faith without the Help of God Himself. Even Jesus said that, without God, He could not do anything. Jesus depended on the operation of faith, by the Holy Spirit while on earth.

Faith that is based on self, cannot survive the onslaught of darkness, neither can it achieve anything significant supernaturally. Willpower is therefore confined to the realm of human possibility while faith in God is operative at the level of the spirit, where what is impossible becomes possible.

"For by grace you have been saved through faith, and that not of yourselves; it is the gift of God, not of works, lest anyone should boast.

For we are His workmanship, created in Christ Jesus for good works, which God prepared beforehand that we should walk in them" (Ephesians 2:8-10)

Salvation Is Received By Faith

Salvation (*Greek–"soteria"*) and everything that it, connotes – preservation, deliverance, safety, prosperity and health – is received by faith. This faith is not a self-generated faith; it is the gift of God. It helps us to understand our dependence and partnership with God. Nonetheless, God has prepared us as His handiwork, for good works.

This means, we have our responsibilities to fulfil. Faith cannot work in us, without God. We are limited, but God is limitless. We are powerless, but God is Most Powerful. It takes God's empowerment in us, to work in supernaturally effective or wonder-working faith.

Therefore, we must see the operation of faith, in reference to the Almighty God and the power of the Holy Spirit. You are not meant to operate faith by yourself, without Him. So, **faith is our spiritual partnership with the invisible God, which empowers us to do the impossible**. All the men of exploit in the Bible, like Moses, Gideon, Abraham, all partnered with God. They were not on their own. Their faith became stronger, as their experience in God became deeper and deeper.

Faith can therefore be considered as "sharing responsibility with God in the light of scriptures so as to have your desired outcome". Faith is taking responsibility. Faith is not waiting for God to work; it is putting God's Word to work. This is the covenant mentality of faith. Faith is personally taking responsibility to do what is required, so that the power of God can be released on one's behalf, to achieve what is desired.

"And a certain man was there, which had an infirmity thirty and eight years. When Jesus saw him lie, and knew that he

had been now a long time in that case, he saith unto him, Wilt thou be made whole? The impotent man answered him, Sir; I have no man, when the water is troubled, to put me into the pool: but while I am coming, another steppeth down before me. Jesus saith unto him, Rise, take up thy bed, and walk. And immediately the man was made whole, and took up his bed, and walked..." (John 5: 5-9)

This man at the pool of Bethesda was waiting for someone to put him into the pool. For thirty-eight years, he was sincere, but sincerely wrong. He was looking outwards, rather than looking inwards – he was looking for solution from the outside. The question that Jesus asked him, was genuinely trying to help him get to the bottom of the problem.

He was asking the man, "how desperate are you, to get your healing..", because he perceived that thirty-eight years was rather too long, not to have come up with a strategy that will allow him to get his healing, even if this depends on help from outside. There is some element of irresponsibility and lack of desperation in how this man presented to Jesus.

Faith is being responsible enough to become desperate to engage the power of God for the solution of your problem. God has given to us all that pertains to life and godliness, through the knowledge of our Lord Jesus Christ. However, we need to add to our faith, other virtues such as, knowledge. This is the responsibility of someone who wants to be established in the faith that conquers; faith that is superior to circumstances.

Sometimes it is common to say "God will do it". If by this statement, it is an acknowledgement of your dependence on God, then, that is alright. However, if it is a statement of "leaving it to God, for God to do whenever He likes", without your involvement, you may find out, that the waiting will be very long, like this man. Don't leave your future to chance. Without active faith, it is impossible to please God. Take responsibility for your faith.

CHAPTER 3

WHERE AND WHEN OF FAITH

Where is faith based? Where does it originate from and from where do we draw from its forces to make it available and applicable to our day to day living? We understand from scriptures that, man exists at three levels, or man has three dimensions of existence and therefore three dimensions of operational base. Man is triune or tripartite.

Just because we have not taken time, to clearly separate these areas of our operational base, and become proficient in accessing the forces resident in all these three domains of our existence does not mean they do not exist. Most people can identify with two of these three parts or bases. Many will no doubt say that man is body and soul.

If we take the body and soul idea, our body cannot generate faith nor does it have the capacity to initiate and operate in faith. If you go with the body and soul concept, then you will say that, faith is at the level of the soul, or something like, faith is in the mind. The mind is able to generate certain extent of hope and believe in what it cannot see. However, as we have seen in earlier discussion, sense-knowledge based faith, which is what the soul or mind can generate is limited in its ability to generate forces beyond the mental or natural realm.

Sense-knowledge based "faith" is at best, mental-agreement, and it can also manifest as willpower. This sort of faith is very limited indeed. It just cannot move the hand of God, neither can it arrest the forces of darkness. Bible faith however, originates and is resident or based in the spirit realm.

The spirit part of man is the base of operation of Bible faith, as opposed to sense-knowledge faith. Bible faith has the capability to release the power of God to deal with any situation, while at the same time can quench all the fiery dart of the enemy, being empowered itself by the power of the Holy Spirit. Bible faith is what this book is about.

The Bible refers to the "spirit, soul and body" of man, as the "whole" aspects of man. According to 1 Thessalonians 5:23, this is the case. There are also other passages of the Bible from where we can draw the same conclusion, but this is beyond the scope of this book. Here, we can see the use of "spirit and soul and body". This means they are three different entities.

"And the very God of peace sanctify you wholly; and I pray God your whole spirit and soul and body be preserved blameless unto the coming of our Lord Jesus Christ." (1 Thessalonians 5:23, KJV)

So, the answer to the question: where is faith? Is that, Bible faith originates from and is resident in the heart of the spirt of man, or better put "in the spirit-man. There is the soul-man, which is made up of the mental or mind aspect of man, together with man's emotion, intellect, and will. It is the psychological part of man. The body-man or the physical-man is the visible part of man.

These three aspects are not individual separate entities of man – they are connected and intertwined. They are like three different points on a circle. Such that, what touches the spirit, affects the soul and body and vice versa of each component.

It is safe to state that, the spirit-soul is invisible, while the body is visible. Man contacts the physical world through his body and part of his senses. Man contacts the spirit realm through his spirit. However, on the basis of Divine creation, Man is primarily a Spirit-being, as he is created after the image and likeness of God (Genesis 1:26-28). **Your spirit man is the God-being inside your human-being.** The soul of man is the seat of mental faculties and awareness. This part links the spirit and the body, to be able to make sense of existence.

So, faith is a spiritual force. One of the fruits of the spirit is faith. (Galatian 5:22) The Holy Spirit dwelling in our spirit is able to produce faith in God. So, in understanding this, it is important to realise that when the Bible refers to the "heart", it is usually referring to the spirit-man, and this is the core but, invisible part or essence of man.

We can see that, the faith that brought salvation is from the heart or the spirit, as the spirit receives enlightenment through the Spoken Word and the work of the Spirt. Bible faith is resident in the heart or spirit of man.

*"But what saith it? The word is nigh thee, even in thy mouth, and in thy heart: that is, the word of faith, which we preach; That if thou shalt confess with thy mouth the Lord Jesus, and shalt believe in thine heart that God hath raised him from the dead, thou shalt be saved. For with the heart man believeth unto righteousness; and with the mouth confession is made unto salvation." (*Romans 10:8-10, KJV)

By faith we contact God, through our spirits because, God is a Spirit. So, we must come to Him and we must worship Him in spirit and in truth.

"God is a Spirit: and they that worship him must worship him in spirit and in truth" (John 4:24).

The same principles of faith for salvation applies to other benefits of the Kingdom in Christ Jesus. The same principles of faith apply throughout the spirit realm – whether it is for salvation or for healing, deliverance from curses or any bondage or addiction, for dealing directly with the forces of darkness, or faith for living a victorious life.

It is the same faith principles that are applied for receiving and walking in the Wisdom from God, or walking in righteousness and holiness. It is the same faith and faith principles that are applicable for operating in divine prosperity or running a business or achievement of academic excellence or family, marriages, children or home. That is why according to divine expectations, the just shall live by the same faith.

When is Faith – The Tense or Timing of Faith?

It is important to talk about the timing of faith or the tense of the same. We can see the closeness and the relationship of these two spiritual forces in the book of Hebrews 11:1

*"Now faith is the **substance** of things hoped for, the **evidence** of things not seen."*

Some authors have put emphasis on the word "Now" signifying the tense of faith, that faith is in present tense, and that hope is in future and that "Now Faith" means faith has to be now. I am not exactly sure that, it is necessary to put any emphasis on the word "now" in order to understand the tense (grammar) or when (timing) of faith.

The two key words here however, point to this without any shadow of doubt.

Hope versus Faith

Hope is an optimistic attitude of mind based on an expectation of positive outcomes related to events and circumstances in one's life. Simply put, hope is positive expectation of the future.

No matter how optimistic, hope will always be in the future. It is not a reality right now. The attitude of hope is a positive attitude, but it is still in the future. There is no way of guaranteeing that the positive future will indeed be realised, but it is a starting point for faith. Without hope for future, there is nothing to base faith on. So hope is important. Hope however, is not faith. Hope cannot reassure us, and hope cannot guarantee anything. So hope alone has no "substance".

Substance (*Greek-hupostasis*) – Substance is "that which has foundation or substructure or actual existence". It is also what supports, the essence or reality of a thing. Substance gives assurance and confidence. Substance is what is tangible or real. Faith is linked to hope. Faith therefore is what gives support, reality, assurance to what is being expected. In other words, **faith transforms hope into what is real**. It makes the future to come to now.

Let's assume I hope to get money to buy a product. Hope is optimistic that the money WILL come, somehow. Faith says, I already have the money now. You cannot say from the blues that you have the money now, without basing your position on a known fact or truth. This is where the Word of God comes into it.

When the expectation for the future (hope) becomes real as if it has already happened – based on God's promises, hope transits into faith. It is no longer a future aspiration, it is a possessed reality. Hope says "I will have it". Faith says, I already have it. Faith is NOW.

Faith is the evidence of things not seen. This completes the picture of what faith is. So, if we extend our analogy a little further. The position of faith is that, I already have the money, based on what God promised me or said to me. The evidence that I have the money is my faith. My faith which is a tangible spiritual force – based on the Word of Promise - is all the evidence I need to have, in order to know that I already have it.

So, faith connects me to what I hope for. Faith forms the basis of my expectation and faith forms the basis of my realisation. If I have faith for it, then I have it. Faith in my heart is all the evidence I need. (Remember that, evidence is knowledge on which to base a belief)

Faith links expectation and evidence of expectation together under one roof, as it were. **Bible faith connects and converts what is expected to what is possessed, even though it is intangible to the physical senses.** It is nonetheless a reality. If it is not now, it is not faith.

Faith speaks of the future, in the present – NOW - as if it is already past. Once I am established in faith for the money that I need to buy my product, I know I already have it. So it is done! If it is done, then it is in the past. I start to speak about already having the money. Remember, in the same way, God calls (NOW) those things that are not (FUTURE), as though they were (PAST). (Romans 4:17).

God declares the future now, as if it is past. Also remember that, faith is resident in the heart, in the realm of the spirit, where time is not a major consideration. Faith also operates, like God, in an eternal NOW - Selah.

Jesus gave us an insight into this type of dealing with that, which is of the spirit and is not tangible. In the book of Mark, He describes the God kind of faith or the faith of God:

"And Jesus answering saith unto them, Have faith in God. For verily I say unto you, That whosoever shall say unto this mountain, Be thou removed, and be thou cast into the sea; and shall not doubt in his heart, but shall believe that those things which he saith shall come to pass; he shall have whatsoever he saith. Therefore I say unto you, what things soever ye desire, when ye pray, believe that ye receive them, and ye shall have them." (Mark 11:22-24)

First, Jesus taught on the power of words – power of speaking the word to an inanimate physical entity, such as a tree or a mountain. He then talks about "believing that you receive." When should you believe you receive them?

"When ye pray". Jesus taught in this particular passage, that **the point of asking in prayer is the point of receiving.** You shall have only those things you believe you received, when you pray. Sometimes, this can be difficult to understand and embrace. How can I believe I have received, when I have not yet seen it happen?

However, this is what faith is about. Anyone can believe what they see with their physical eyes or what they perceive with their senses. Asking in faith, in prayer, is almost like a spiritual transaction – you bring faith, to purchase – say, a desire, goal or need, which has scriptural foundation. When you release the faith, the desired is also released back to you in turn.

Faith is the currency of the spirit realm. All these are spiritual transactions. We must now translate this into a physical manifestation. Let me share with you how the Lord opened my eyes to see this. How do you translate what you have received in the spirit into physical manifestation?

The Holy Spirit used the salvation experience to explain the principles of faith. Faith is faith, whether it is used for salvation, healing, prosperity or the salvation of a nation. It is the same faith, in operation.

Faith for Salvation

A Principle of Faith for All Needs

We have established the truth that we are saved by grace through faith, according to Ephesians 2:8. We also know that, the Bible tells us that, at salvation we received (by impartation) a measure of faith (Romans 12:3). How did this faith come, how was it imparted?

"How then shall they call on him in whom they have not believed? And how shall they believe in him of whom they have not heard? And how shall they hear without a preacher? So then faith cometh by hearing, and hearing by the word of God." (Romans 10:14, 17)

We can see here that faith for salvation came because, someone was sent to preach the gospel of salvation. We heard the Word – the good news that God so loves the world that he gave His only begotten Son, Jesus Christ and that, if we believe in Him, we can be saved. (John 3:16). In this story that involved Nicodemus, Jesus said, you must be born again. Jesus then explained, in response to Nicodemus' question that, He wasn't talking about natural birth, but spiritual birth (new spiritual reference point, in the same way a baby is given a physical reference point at birth).

In receiving the message of salvation, we perceived the Love of God. We also understood that we cannot save ourselves and that our good works will not be enough to save us (Isaiah 64:6; Romans 3:20; Galatians 2:16).

We heard and believed that Jesus Christ is the Way, the Truth and the Life, and that, no one can come to the Father, except by Him (John 14:6). We heard that it is appointed to man to die once and after this judgement (Hebrews 9:27). We appreciate the fact that all have sinned and come short of the glory of God, but that, the gift of God is eternal life. (Romans 3:23-24) God does not want any man to perish, but that all should come to repentance and receive the gift of eternal life (2 Peter 3:9). We were informed that, if we ask Jesus to forgive us and save us, He is faithful and just to do so (1 John 1:8-10).

These truth drew our hearts to the Lord. I am sure, not everyone heard the gospel preached to them exactly in that way. However, for everyone who is a born-again Christian, there is always something that drew them to say "Yes" to the Good News of Salvation, through our Lord Jesus Christ. According to Romans 10:17, faith for salvation came by hearing this message or the Word of God, concerning salvation.

Having heard, we responded based on what we have believed about the Good News and then, we prayed the "prayer of salvation". Majority of the time, prayer of salvation is based on recognition of Romans 10:8-10, and this prayer highlights some of the principles of faith, which we will mention now, but discuss in more details later.

"But the righteousness of faith speaks in this way, "Do not say in your heart, 'Who will ascend into heaven?'" (That is, to bring Christ down from above) or, "'who will descend into the abyss?'"(That is, to bring Christ up from the dead). But what does it say? "The word is near you, in your mouth and in your heart" (that is, the word of faith which we preach): that if you confess with your mouth the Lord Jesus and believe in your heart that God has raised Him from the dead, you will be saved. For with the heart one believes unto righteousness, and with the mouth confession is made unto salvation."

It does say that, the Word is near the person needing salvation – the Word (of faith) is in the mouth and in the heart. That if we confess with our **mouth** the Lord Jesus, and we believe, with our **heart**, that God raised Him from the dead, we will be saved. This is because, we need to **believe with the heart**, to be made right, and we need to **confess or declare with the mouth** to experience salvation. This is the biblical process, whether it happens in church, alone, on the street, in a small church or on crusade ground, on the hospital bed, or wherever – it is the same.

Let's do a little exercise here. The word "saved" or "salvation" also included the idea of healing, preservation, prosperity, deliverance, soundness, rescue from danger or injury and being made whole. Therefore, it will be correct to substitute the word salvation for any of these implied meaning of "saved" or "salvation", as follows:

"..That if we CONFESS with our MOUTH the Lord Jesus, and we BELIEVE, with our HEART, that God raised Him form the dead, we will be healed, preserved, delivered, made sound, rescued from danger, made whole or prosper!"

This means that in order to receive healing, deliverance, wholeness, well-being including prosperity, you need to do two things – **BELIEVE WITH THE HEART AND CONFESS WITH THE MOUTH.** What do you believe and confess? You believe what the Word of God says about the issue and declare with the mouth what God has said.

Immediate Result and Salvation, Now!

"In an acceptable time I have heard you, and in the day of salvation I have helped you." Behold, **now** *is the accepted time; behold, now is the day of salvation." (2 Corinthians 6:2)*

When you prayed the prayer of salvation, you believed that God answered you straight away. You are declared "saved". You did not necessarily feel saved, but you walked away, being told you were saved. Why? Because we are easy to believe for the salvation, which is of the spirit or which is spiritual.

However when it comes to other "salvations" – salvation from sickness and disease, or salvation from demonic oppression or salvation from poverty and lack, somehow, we have a problem believing or declaring that it has already happened, even if we cannot see, feel, touch or taste it with our physical senses.

The Spirit of the Lord showed me that, the same way we received salvation by faith, is the same way that we need to receive all the redemption rights and privileges, by faith. First it has to be in the heart, through believing the Word of faith concerning the covenant right, then based on this, we declare with the mouth about the same issue or right. Once we have done, this, **it is done.**

I believe very much according to Scriptures that, initial salvation experience is a supernatural event, a definite operation of the spirit and the angelic hosts, which takes place when someone receives salvation. The scripture says there is a taking away of the heart of stone and replacement with the heart of the flesh (Ezekiel 36:26, 27).

It also says that, angels do rejoice in heaven, when someone comes to, repents and confesses the Lord to be saved. (Luke 12: 8; Luke 15:10).

This simple operation of faith (for salvation), based on the Word, of God, of believing in the heart and confessing with the mouth, provokes the activities of the spirit realm and the involvement of the angelic hosts and the release of the miraculous power of the Holy Spirit! Meanwhile, nothing much might have necessarily changed (visibly) in the soul-mind and body of man.

Similarly, **WE MUST BELIEVE** that, it is the same simple operation of faith (for healing, deliverance, preservation, prosperity or well-being), based on the Word, of believing in the heart and confessing with the mouth, (regarding the healing, deliverance, preservation, prosperity or well-being), that provokes the activities of the spirit realm and the involvement of the angels, and the release of the miraculous power of the Holy Spirit!

It is a heavenly spiritual reality, similar to the salvation from sin and eternal damnation. It the same way, that healing, deliverance, wholeness and well-being is imparted in the spirit realm, immediately the believing and the confession has taken place.

Believing the Invisible

Manifesting Inner Reality

It is interesting to note that, after the prayer of salvation, there is a period of seeking reassurance of salvation, spiritual growth and engagement in activities that will lead to establishment of the faith. This often involves studying the Bible, developing a prayer and personal relationship with God, attending worship service in a Bible believing church, water baptism, baptism in the Holy Spirit with the evidence of speaking in tongues, a walk of righteous living and developing friendship with those who are already in the faith.

All these in no time, result in visible evidence of the salvation, which at first was just a spiritual experience. It soon evidently develops into a way of life, reflecting the character of Christ. What has happened here is that, by believing and engaging with that which is an invisible experience of salvation, the new believer, has learnt how to visibly manifest the inner reality.

It is important to note that, in most cases, if you ask, whether the new believer is saved or not, if they understood what has taken place, they will declare very firmly that they are saved. If you ask if they are going to heaven, they will also positively affirm that they are. This continues through the years in the faith. The Word of Salvation and the spiritual experience of salvation has become manifest in their lives.

When it comes to healing, deliverance, soundness, and other expression of salvation, we often then take a very different view. We tend not to believe that healing has been received until, it is manifested. The same principles of faith applies to all areas. We sometimes tend to vigorously doubt if anything has taken place, in the realm of the spirit, when we prayed the prayer of faith for healing. For example, just because we cannot see.

However, we need to realise that, in the same way that faith provokes and maintains a spiritual response when someone believes in the heart and confesses with the mouth concerning salvation, similarly, the same spiritual response is provoked when someone who is sick, unwell or who is in one form of bondage or the other, believes in their heart and confesses with the mouth their healing or deliverance. The impartation and healing is immediate in the realm of the spirit. The healing is NOW!

We must learn that, in the same way that, the person who has been saved can say that she/he is saved, based on the Word of God, rather than on the visible change in character, we must be able to confidently declare our healing based solely on the Word of God, and our understanding of the principles of faith and what is going on in the spiritual realm, concerning that healing or deliverance or desire.

In the next chapter, we will look more closely at the fact that, faith is a spiritual force, which is dynamic and tangible and reliable. Faith provokes the power of God to be released on our behalf, and this spiritual power interfaces and interacts with the natural, spiritual, mental or physical forces that is required to manifest our miracle.

What we must learn to do, is to engage with all those things that will enhance the manifestation of healing (or whatever we are believing God for), in the same way we approach the salvation experience.

This means that regarding healing for example, once you have believed in your heart and declared with your mouth, you go back to the Word, and be reassured about the healing, continue to declare the healing you have received and associate with people who are also positive in faith and be encouraged, observe healthy options, continue to relate personally with God and through the Holy Spirit, receive from Him the direction that He wants you to follow for the healing to manifest.

Like in water baptism or baptism with the Holy Spirit, you may need to have someone or an elder or pastor agree and pray over you, the prayer of faith (James 5:14-15), anointing you with oil, as opportunity to release your faith through these modes of spiritual impartation of virtue.

However, there must never be any time, in which you start to doubt the healing, in your heart (inner self – not necessarily in your head). Never must you speak contrary to the healing that you have received. Then you must act healed, in the same way that you act, as someone who is saved. These are general guiding principles that can be adapted to anything we are standing for in faith.

We find the scriptural basis, believe in the heart, declare with the mouth, and then believe we have received and then do what needs to the done, by works to see the manifestation – whether it happens slowly or quickly, there must never be a time we doubt, in our heart, that we have received the answer.

Now let's learn about the spiritual forces behind the scene, which are at work, through operations of faith, bringing to pass the desired goal(s).

CHAPTER 4

THE FORCE OF FAITH?

To understand by revelation, the importance of the force of faith, let's review the practical definition of faith, perhaps put together one unified definition that will incorporate the various aspects that we have looked at so far. We have already established the fact that there are two worlds that are very real – although one is visible (physical) and the other is invisible (spiritual). The truth is that, faith is a tangible spiritual force

"Faith is the unreserved responsible display of confidence in God, that causes one to act and declare, based on being fully persuaded in one's heart that God's Word is true, despite the fact that prevailing circumstances may be contrary: not changing one's position until the desired result, which is in line with the Word, becomes fully manifested."

This kind of faith provokes a response or reaction in the unseen realm of the spirit, moving the hand of God to **forcefully** effect the required change and stopping the hand of the enemy from being able to interfere, interrupt or hinder the manifestation of the desired result. This forceful effect is what is often manifested as the supernatural or the miraculous, where what is naturally or humanly impossible becomes possible. **The exercise of faith provokes the release of force in the unseen spirit realm**. This force generated by faith is designed and targeted towards the achievement of the original intention, purpose or desired goal of faith. Let us define what a force is.

"A **force** is a push or pull upon an object resulting from the object's *interaction* with another object. Whenever there is an *interaction* between two objects, there is a force upon each of the objects. When the *interaction* ceases, the two objects no longer experience the force. Forces only exist as a result of an interaction". - Farlex Web Free Dictionary

From this description of "force", we can see that, forces always exist as a result of interaction. The force of faith is no exception. Faith generates a force in the spirit, which begins to interact with the situation that needs to change. Faith releases the power that is operative against any spiritual or physical resistance. It compels or restrains its target, to conform to the demands of faith.

Degrees of Faith

As we will discuss in more detail later, there are various degrees or levels of faith. It is the level of faith that determines both the extent and the speed of the outcome.

For example **"no faith"** level is unlikely to generate any result that is only achievable based on God's Word. **"Little faith"** will be able to generate some spiritual force, but will not be able to achieve the same result as **"the gift of faith"**. So our faith should be ever-increasing, as we master the principles and laws that makes faith to be effective.

Invisible Forces

To help us to be able to imagine and see what is happening in the realm of the spirit concerning the force of faith, please note that, in the world of science and nature, forces do not need to be seen to be believed.

"The wind blows where it wishes, and you hear the sound of it, but cannot tell where it comes from and where it goes. So is everyone who is born of the Spirit." (John 3:8)

There is a force generated by wind. Although you cannot see it, - it is an invisible force – it does however generate visible effect, seen as the movement of trees, blowing of loose objects. The force of the wind, in its highly focused state, can result in tornadoes which are powerful enough to clear a whole building out of its way. This is still an invisible force, with visible effects.

Force of gravity is another invisible force, which is always in operation. For example, we are kept in the standing, erect position, by the force of gravity. If there is no force of gravity in operation, as for example in Space, it is not possible to stand and walk in the erect position. This is another invisible yet powerful force. You do not need to see the force itself, to believe in the existence of the force of gravity.

There are yet other forces, such as electromagnetic force or, the nuclear force. These are invisible, yet powerful forces. Their effects cannot be denied, when in operation. So also is the force of faith. It is not visible, but when it is in operation, its effect(s) cannot be denied.

The Force of Faith is backed by the Power of the Holy Spirit

Please be reminded that, the force of faith is not a force of self-faith, or willpower but is backed by the power of the Holy Spirit, dwelling in our spirit. The degree of the spiritual force of faith that is generated in individual believer's life, is directly related to the measure of the power of the Holy Spirit that is at work in the life of that believer. That is why it is important to build spiritual strength, in the operation of faith.

"In the beginning God created the heavens and the earth. The earth was without form, and void; and darkness was on the face of the deep. And the Spirit of God was hovering over the face of the waters. Then God said, "Let there be light"; and there was light." (Genesis 1:1-3)

The Spirit of God is always "hovering over", awaiting the Word of Faith to be released, and He swings into creative action, according to the "power level".

"Now to Him who is able to do exceedingly abundantly above all that we ask or think, according to the power that works in us," (Ephesians 3:20)

Manifestation is always according to the level of the Power of God that is resident and operative inside us. The reason is that, our faith is not in isolation but, it is based upon the Word of God. So the Holy Spirit is the source and the guarantor: He is the Power behind the force, because the Holy Spirit confirms the Word

"And they went out and preached everywhere, the Lord working with them and confirming the word through the accompanying signs. Amen." (Mark 16:20).

Also, Jesus confirmed this in some of His "last words" – that the Holy Spirit will confirm the Word:

"However, when He, the Spirit of truth, has come, He will guide you into all truth; for He will not speak on His own authority, but whatever He hears He will speak; and He will tell you things to come." (John 16:13).

The gift of faith for example, is the manifestation of the Holy Spirit given for our profit. So we will always need the ministry of the Holy Spirit in the operation of faith.

"But the manifestation of the Spirit is given to each one for the profit of all: for to one is given the word of wisdom through the Spirit, to another the word of knowledge through the same Spirit, to another faith by the same Spirit, to another gifts of healings by the same Spirit," (1 Corinthian 12:7-9)

Force of Faith in Operation

Now let's look at a few examples of the force of faith in operation. Behind many miracles or supernatural manifestations is the force of faith. It is important to put your "imagination cap" on, so you can receive an impartation of the Spirit, as we look at these examples. I want you to then imagine the same force of faith at work in the area that you are believing God for. Whatever is going to take to manifest your heart desire, see the force of faith, actively working on it to effect the necessary changes.

The Force of Faith can reverse the process of Death

"Jesus saith unto her, Said I not unto thee, that, if thou wouldest believe, thou shouldest see the glory of God?" (John 11:40 KJV)

In this story, Jesus' comment above can be literary translated as: "**Did I not say to you that if you would have** faith, you would see the glory of God"? Jesus then went ahead and demonstrated His Faith, by asking them to role away the stone and calling Lazarus forth, from the region of the dead, despite being dead for four days and stinking.

Now when He had said these things, He cried with a loud voice, "Lazarus, come forth!" And he who had died came out bound hand and foot with grave clothes, and his face was wrapped with a cloth. Jesus said to them, "Loose him, and let him go."

Faith power or the Force of Faith (and the Anointing of the Holy Spirit) was and is still able to reverse and restore the process of death and death itself. For Lazarus to have been brought back from death, there would have been a spiritual force in operation which was interacting with the spirit and soul and body of Lazarus. The force of faith would have arrested the spirit and the eternal soul component of Lazarus and force it to return back to his body.

The same supernatural invisible force would have kick-started the heart, liquefy the blood in his blood circulation (or vascular) system and restore all the blood vessels, the organs, the brain functions, the muscle and bone functions for him to have been able to get up from the grave and started walking out.

The operation of faith (and the Anointing of the Holy Spirit) would have in this instant moment reclaimed the spirit life of Lazarus, restore it back to his body and instantly revive all the body systems and empower the previously dead Lazarus to get on his feet and walk. Hallelujah! Amen! All these, taking place is an instant, by the power of the Holy Spirit, released, through the force of faith

The Force of Faith can stop the great Storm

The force of faith can invade the invisible world of the physical - and stop or overcome the contrary or adversarial force that was driving the storm or the raging sea, again in an instant.

"And there arose a great storm of wind, and the waves beat into the ship, so that it was now full. And he arose, and rebuked the wind, and said unto the sea, Peace, be still. And the wind ceased, and there was a great calm. And he said unto them, why are ye so fearful? How is it that ye have no faith?" (Mark 4:37-40)

Jesus' comment here is very insightful. It gave us the understanding of how Jesus was thinking and what He did and why, in addressing the unforeseen circumstances that developed during their voyage. Jesus was thinking – "Well, we are going to the other side, that is where we are going, nothing is going to stop us from getting there – not even this storm. Now, I have power over this storm, and this storm is going to have to obey my command. It has already done some damage, so I am going to have to stop it immediately". He most certainly believed that His Word carries Power and that He Himself has authority.

So He released His Word, being fully persuaded that it will not return to Him without accomplishing the purpose, for which it is being released. So He spoke to the storm and commanded it to stop. He didn't pray to God to stop the storm, He simply ordered it to stop. **Jesus simply ordered the storm to stop**. To show that it was by faith that He calmed the storm, He rebuked the disciples, in correcting and training them on the principles of faith.

First, why are you afraid? To even think you were going to die, is not faith. FEAR – is False Evidence Appearing Real. Secondly, why did you not exercise any faith at all, in your power to challenge and subdue the power of this storm, by the force of faith? He was expecting them to do so, but they didn't, rather they were panicking and speaking word of unbelief, words of fear. Notice and imagine, that when Jesus spoke that Word of faith in command to the storm, the force of faith went into operation and resisted the wind and overpowered it.

The word "ceased" (*Greek - kopazo*) here is very insightful. "Kopazo" means to grow weary and tired. In order words, the force of faith mounted up so much counter-force against the wind, such that the strength of the wind (storm) could not overpower the force of faith, and it became "tired out". Faith is a tangible spiritual force! It tires out all the opposition of darkness, and subdue their kingdom operations, so you can receive the end result of your faith.

The Force of Faith can Stop Abnormal Menstrual Bleeding

It is generally believed that, the woman with "an issue of blood" described in the ministry of Jesus had a long-standing abnormal irregular or continuous menstrual bleeding, which for some reason could not be stopped, despite several medical intervention and significant financial loss. However, it could also have been an abnormal bleeding from any surface of the body.

"And a certain woman, which had an issue of blood twelve years, And had suffered many things of many physicians, and had spent all that she had, and was nothing bettered, but rather grew worse, For she said, If I may touch but his clothes, I shall be whole. And straightway the fountain of her blood was dried up; and she felt in her body that she was healed of that plague. And he said unto her, Daughter, thy faith hath made thee whole; go in peace, and be whole of thy plague." (Mark 5:25-34)

The first thing to note in this true story is that – **this woman scheduled her miracle – she decided and declared that she was going to touch the hem of Jesus' garment,** and that she was going to be made whole. He didn't even ask Jesus, what His opinion was!

The second lesson is that it was through the operation of faith that the woman was able to command and initiate the flow of healing power. The release of faith, also simultaneously released the power of God on her behalf. The force of faith effected her instantaneous healing.

Can you remember our first definition of faith? We said that **"Faith is the Spiritual Medium through which we tap into the power of the Almighty God."** It's the channel that connects us to the flow of the Power of God for a change of situation.

It helps us to tap into virtue for our desired change. This woman tapped into the Power of the Almighty God, at work in the life of Jesus Christ. She connected to the flow of God's Power, for a change of situation – the healing of her long-standing medical problem. Virtue was released by the force of faith and this virtue also went inside the woman's body to correct the abnormal bleeding, in an instant.

The force of faith would have surged through the affected part and immediately sealed all the sources of bleeding and at the same time corrected the hormonal imbalance and blood clotting abnormality that this woman might have developed. The force of faith was able to flow through the body of the woman with an issue of blood, and stopped the flow of blood - correct whatever needs to be corrected for the flow to cease.

Jesus categorically said, it was her faith that made her whole. She heard the good news of the healing Jesus. This imparted faith in her, and she then decided herself, both HOW and WHEN she was going to be healed! She did not wait for anybody (including Jesus) to tell her when she was going to be healed.

She released her faith in that, whenever she touched the hem of Jesus garment, she WILL - not might - be made whole. She went and did just that, by faith; and this gave her the miracle she had been looking for. Praise God! You can do the same.

The Force of Faith Restores Nerves, Muscles and Tendons

"And a certain man lame from his mother's womb was carried, whom they laid daily at the gate of the temple which is called Beautiful, to ask alms of them that entered into the temple;" (Acts 3:2) "Then Peter said, Silver and gold have I none; but such as I have give I thee: In the name of Jesus Christ of Nazareth rise up and walk." (Acts 3:6) "And his name through faith in his name hath made this man strong, whom ye see and know: yea, the faith which is by him hath

given him this perfect soundness in the presence of you all." (Acts 3:16).

This story confirmed that this man has never walked. Peter had developed and renewed his confidence in the resurrected Christ. Faith in the Name of Jesus, was what brought that confidence. He had seen Jesus at work in the miraculous.

He had learnt some principles of faith. He knew that faith worked. Even if he wasn't sure whether His own faith would be sufficient for the healing of this man, he was certain that the faith of Jesus would.

In addition, since Jesus had given them both power and authority, to act on His behalf, he was confident that he would obtain result on behalf of this man. We see that, the force of faith in the power, authority and ability of Jesus became effective, as this spiritual force went inside the muscles, nerves, tendon and bone, to be restored.

Crippled Man Restored by the Force of Faith

Another story, where the force of faith went into operation for the manifestation of healing is seen in this story of the crippled man at Lystra, who also experienced the power of faith, where the force generated by this power, penetrated the damaged muscles, tendon, nerves bones and all that was necessary to totally restore this man's feet.

"And there sat a certain man at Lystra, impotent in his feet, being a cripple from his mother's womb, who never had walked.

The same heard Paul speak: who steadfastly beholding him, and perceiving that he had faith to be healed, said with a loud voice, Stand upright on thy feet.

And he leaped and walked. And when the people saw what Paul had done, they lifted up their voices, saying in the speech of Lycaonia, The gods are come down to us in the likeness of men." (Acts 14:8-1, KJV)

The force of faith puts the believer in a position to operate, in the realm of the supernatural - in the realm or class of God.

The Force of Faith Qualifies You for a Miracle

This is a really very moving testimony of the power and the force of faith.

Here we see that, the persistence in faith, despite opposition, hopelessness, disqualification, can move the hand of mercy towards you, even when you do not qualify.

The Force of Faith is your qualifier for the supernatural. Here we learn about the display of "great faith". Let's learn from putting together the two accounts of the incident, from the Gospel according to Saint Mark and Saint Matthew.

"For a certain woman, whose young daughter had an unclean spirit, heard of him, and came and fell at his feet: The woman was a Greek, a Syrophenician by nation; and she besought him that he would cast forth the devil out of her daughter." (Mark 7: 25-28)

"But he answered her not a word. And his disciples came and besought him, saying, Send her away; for she crieth after us. - But he answered and said, it is not meet to take the children's bread, and to cast it to dogs. And she said, Truth, Lord: yet the dogs eat of the crumbs which fall from their masters' table. Then Jesus answered and said unto her, O woman, great is thy faith: be it unto thee even as thou wilt. And her daughter was made whole from that very hour." (Matthew 15:23-28)

The disciples were going to send her away, and Jesus agreed that, she was not qualified for the power flow from Jesus to her daughter, neither was Jesus also ready to operate in faith for the deliverance and the healing of this lady's daughter.

Jesus also was not sent to her in His earthly ministry. She was a Greek, and therefore, a Gentile, which disqualified her. Jesus even compared her to a dog, calling her a dog, directly to her face. But this did not stop her operation of faith, for her miracle. Her faith qualified her, and she received her miracle.

In the same way, your faith will qualify you for what you want but you are not entitled to. Jesus described this as an example of Great Faith. Can you imagine, Jesus said, "Be it unto you as thou wilt." In other words, Jesus was saying "because of my assignment, I am really not particularly minded to heal your daughter, but since you want it, and you are standing in faith for it, I cannot deny you, so, I lock my faith with your faith and let it be according to your heart' desire, dear lady". Wow. **Faith will move the hand of favour toward you today, even if you do not qualify, for whatever reason.**

The Force of Faith Causes You to Overcome

Regardless of the odd stack against you, it is through the force of faith that your situation will become turned around from failure to success, from defeat to victory. The Force of Faith literally goes into operation, to begin to alter the outcome in your favour. Faith is the Victory that overcomes all adversities. You are coming out of everything that binds or hinders your destiny in Jesus' Name.

"For whatever is born of God overcometh the world; and this is the victory that overcometh the world, even our faith." Who

is he that overcometh the world, but he that believeth that Jesus is the Son of God." (1 John 5:4-5 KJV)

The Spirit of Faith Generating the Force of Faith

It is important to reiterate the role and the ministry of the Holy Spirt on the human spirit. Faith of the heart speaks, the spirit of faith speaks. He thinks the Word and speaks the Word

"We having the same spirit of faith, according as it is written, I believed, and therefore have I spoken; we also believe, and therefore speak" (2 Corinthians 4:13)

A man's belly shall be satisfied with the fruit of his mouth; and with the increase of his lips shall he be filled. Death and life are in the power of the tongue: and they that love it shall eat the fruit thereof." (Proverbs 18:20-21)

"A good man out of the good treasure of the heart bringeth forth good things: and an evil man out of the evil treasure bringeth forth evil things. But I say unto you, that every idle word that men shall speak, they shall give account thereof in the Day of Judgment. For by thy words thou shalt be justified, and by thy words thou shalt be condemned." (Matthew 12:35-37)

The kingdom heroes operated with the spirit of faith. David killed Goliath by the spirit of faith. Daniel's faith shut the mouth of the lion. The three Hebrew children, by the spirit of faith took a stand not to bow down to golden idols of the King.

Ezekiel Prophesied to dry bones by the spirit of faith. Jesus and the disciples by the spirit of faith cast out devils, calmed storms and raised the dead. The common expression of the spirit of faith, is that the spirit of faith speaks.

They spoke what they were convinced of, but it is the Holy Spirit that empowered them to be so confident. By faith they subdued kingdoms. Faith indeed, is the master key to the world of dominion.

CHAPTER 5

CHARACTERISTICS OF EFFECTIVE FAITH

What are the characteristics of the faith that wins or works? What are the characteristics of effective faith? In the book of Hebrews, in chapter 11, we have a catalogue of people who walked by faith in God and we see the various exploits accomplished by these people. What are the things that made their operation of faith stand out, and more importantly achieve their desired goal?

The following chapter of Hebrews (chapter 12), in summarising the learning points from these patriarchs, referred to them as "cloud of witnesses". These patriarchs of faith have themselves been witnesses to the power of faith in that, they can attest or affirm to the effectiveness or values of walking by faith.

They are now looking and watching us from heaven, expecting that, in the same way that they have made it, we will also make it in faith. They are our reference points in faith towards God. That is why we are being encouraged and inspired to "run the race that is set before us" with steadfastness, constancy and endurance.

We are expected to turn our eyes away from other things and fix them on Jesus, who is the chief leader, who takes the lead and is the pioneer of our faith, acting as perfect and highest examples for us to follow. (Hebrews 12:1-3).

Faith is a radical virtue that is so laser-focused on its goal that, nothing can deter it from continuing, until the desired result is achieved. In the case of Jesus, He endured the cross, He despised the shame, the oppositions that He faced and He refused to be weary or tire out, until He achieved the purpose of the Cross and now that He has accomplished His task, He is sat down, at the right hand of the throne of God. Well done! It's worth it!

"Winning Faith" is "Dominion Faith" – the faith for dominion that causes us to be in charge, on top and in control, no matter what. So let's look at the five characteristics of this enduring faith that constantly achieves the tasks that are set before it:

Winning Faith Is Word-Based Faith

The Word of God is the foundation for effective faith. As we have discussed before, Bible faith is not self-faith and it is not mental faith, it is not will-power. The origin of this faith is the Word of God – it is Word-founded. It is also engaged and steered by the Word of God. This means that, it is enwrapped, involved, driven directed and navigated by the Word of God.

"So then, faith cometh by hearing, and hearing by the word of God." (Romans 10:17)

Now, the Word of God is the Will of God. Faith in God's Word is faith in God Himself, because:

"In the beginning was the Word, and the Word was with God, and the Word was God. He was in the beginning with God. All things were made through Him, and without Him nothing was made that was made. In Him was life, and the life was the light of men. And the light shines in the darkness, and the darkness did not comprehend it." (John 1:1-5)

God is a loving God. His Word has been given to us, as a guide to life and living. The Word is like a manual for life. To get the best of a product, the manual is produced to help guide the person who purchases the product to know the ins and outs of the product, to understand how it works, different features and the "dos" and "don'ts" and also what to do in case of problem or malfunction and how to ensure that the consumer enjoys the product, maintain and value it.

Similarly, the Word of God is His manual, provided over centuries of existence of Man, to help guide us, instructing us on how best to live, helps us to know the ins and outs of life, to understand how life works, to know the different features and what matters and the "dos" and "don'ts" of life and also what to do when problems or crises arise in the journey of life.

The Word helps us to deal with life's failure and how to ensure that we enjoy and value life, as God intends. In the same way that a manufacturer creates a product, with a reason or purpose in mind, God has created us with purpose and intent and the fulfilment of life, is when the life is lived according to Divine intentions.

"All Scripture is given by inspiration of God, and is profitable for doctrine, for reproof, for correction, for instruction in righteousness, that the man of God may be complete, thoroughly equipped for every good work." (2 Timothy 3:16-17)

So, when faith is based on the Word of God, it is based on and backed by God Himself. It forms the basis of expectation and it draws directly from the faithfulness and integrity of God Himself. The Word of God is designed to produce and prosper the believer, as we have learnt from Isaiah 55:10-11.

"For as the rain comes down, and the snow from heaven, And do not return there, But water the earth, And make it bring forth and bud, That it may give seed to the sower And bread to the eater, So shall My word be that goes forth from My mouth; It shall not return to me void, But it shall

accomplish what I please, And it shall prosper in the thing for which I sent it."

If God's Word is true, then it must produce, according to this scripture. Therefore as a believer, it is important for you to settle down and be convinced on the integrity of God's Word, as contained in the Bible. **If you are in doubt about the integrity or the validity of God's Word, your faith in the Word cannot blossom.**

The Word cannot produce for you, if you doubt it. If you do not believe that a product works for something, it is doubtful whether you will ever buy it or use it, for that thing. The Word of God, is not for trial and error. It is for doing.

"God is not a man, that He should lie, nor a son of man, that He should repent. Has He said, and will He not do? Or has He spoken, and will He not make it good?" (Numbers 23:19)

"My covenant I will not break, nor alter the word that has gone out of my lips. Once I have sworn by my holiness; I will not lie to David" (Psalms 89:34-35)

God is not a liar. Should the Almighty God, even have to say this to anyone, at all? We however, many times make Him out to be a liar, concerning His promises. This is why the children of Israel, who came out of Egypt, could not truly enjoy the great benefits of having the Almighty God, as their God. They were so often very doubtful of Him and His Word.

"For indeed the gospel was preached to us as well as to them; but the word which they heard did not profit them not being mixed with faith in those who heard it" (Hebrews 4:2).

As the saying goes – "God said it, I believe it and that settles it". The Word of God is settled whether we believe or not, but this saying helps to reinforce the fact that, the Word of God, which is God's position on the matter is final.

It should not be contested, argued against or come as second consideration. The Word of God should be Number One, and it will only profit those who exalt it and mix it with faith. So, winning faith is usually based and established on what God has said, in His Word. God's Word supersedes any report, analysis, natural force, spiritual entities or human opinion. Wining faith agrees entirely with God's Word.

"For what if some did not believe? Will their unbelief make the faithfulness of God without effect? Certainly not! Indeed, let God be true but every man a liar" (Romans 3:3-4a)

The admonition of Hebrews 6:12-20 cannot be any clearer regarding the need to trust and rely on the Word, and that is, God's Word. For ease of understanding, I have presented this in the New Century Version (NCV).

"We do not want you to become lazy. Be like those who through faith and patience will receive what God has promised. God made a promise to Abraham. And as there is no one greater than God, he used himself when he swore to

Abraham, saying, "I will surely bless you and give you many descendants Abraham waited patiently for this to happen, and he received what God promised.

People always use the name of someone greater than themselves when they swear. The oath proves that what they say is true, and this ends all arguing. God wanted to prove that his promise was true to those who would get what he promised. And he wanted them to understand clearly that his purposes never change, so he made an oath. These two things cannot change: God cannot lie when he makes a promise, and he cannot lie when he makes an oath. These things encourage us who came to God for safety. They give us strength to hold on to the hope we have been given.

We have this hope as an anchor for the soul, sure and strong. It enters behind the curtain in the Most Holy Place in heaven, where Jesus has gone ahead of us and for us. He has become the high priest forever, a priest like Melchizedek." *(Hebrews 6:12-10, NCV).*

For emphasis, the verses say - God cannot lie when He makes a promise, and He cannot lie when He makes an oath. These things encourage us who come to God for safety. They give us strength to hold on to the hope we have been given. We have this hope as an anchor for the soul, sure and strong. Our minds, intellect, will and emotions desire an anchor (assurance), and this anchor can be derived from trusting in the Word of God, as infallible, reliable and trustworthy. Be encouraged today, to stand on the living Word of the Living God.

We have already seen that Abraham's faith was based on the Word of promise that God gave him, which God reconfirmed several times.

(Genesis 12, Genesis 15 and Genesis 17). Similarly Sarah's faith was based on what God had promised (His Word)

"By faith Sarah herself also received strength to conceive seed, and she bore a child when she was past the age, because she judged Him faithful who had promised." (Hebrews 11:11).

We also see an instance where King Jehoshaphat recalled God's Word of promise (to their forefathers) in prayer, when faced with a national crises, which could have led to their destruction, as in 2 Chronicles 20: 1-10. This faith is Word-based.

Winning Faith Is Revelation-Based Faith

It is one thing to know that you must base your faith on God's Word; it's another thing to have an understanding of the Word, on which you are basing your expectation, and how this Word applies to you. Revelation-fired faith is based on understanding; and spiritual understanding is a booster of faith.

"So Philip ran to him, and heard him reading the prophet Isaiah, and said, "Do you understand what you are reading?" And he said, "How can I, unless someone guides me?" And he asked Philip to come up and sit with him."

"Then Philip opened his mouth, and began at the same scripture, and preached unto him Jesus." And as they went on their way, they came unto a certain water: and the eunuch said, See, here is water; what doth hinder me to be baptized?" And Philip said, If thou believest with all thine heart, thou mayest. And he answered and said, I believe that Jesus Christ is the Son of God." (Acts 8: 30-31; 35-37)

If you reflect on this passage with Romans 10:8-17 in mind, you will come to the conclusion that Phillip opened the understanding of the scriptures to the Ethiopian eunuch, which allowed him to receive an impartation of faith for his salvation. He received a revelation of the salvation message and this caused him to be driven toward accepting Jesus Christ, as the Messiah and then going on to become water baptised.

As we have discussed before, "Revelation" (*Greek - apokalupsis*) means an unveiling, a disclosure or making visible of things which before then was not visible. We used the example of revelation, as what happened when the king sent a warrant of arrest for Prophet Elisha, who was on the mountain, following an accusation of conspiracy, to undermine the king's military defence.

The servant of the prophet was afraid, as he felt quite helpless. Elisha asked that God will open his spiritual eyes, so that he can base his faith and reassurance for Divine Security and Divine Protection on this revelation.

"And he answered, Fear not: for they that be with us are more than they that be with them."

Let's assume you are just reading this or remember this scenario at a time, when you are facing a great opposition and it appears that the opposition is closing in on you, the Spirit of God, may suddenly highlight this Truth in your spirit, telling you and reassuring you, not to worry, not to be moved, by reason of the great multitude. You suddenly "see" what Elisha's servant saw, in the spirit realm, and your faith is energised. This is revelation. You will also most likely declare:

"Yes, I am not going to be moved, because God is on my side, I will not be afraid, because those that are with me are more than they that are with them. Greater is He who is in me than he that is in the world."

This is a revelation-fired winning faith. We learnt that when our faith is based on this kind of revelation, ("unveiling"), it is difficult to doubt the existence of that which one has seen. This is the beginning of winning or dominion faith! Faith begins when the revealed truth of God's Word, concerning a matter is known.

The Holy Spirit is the master facilitator of revelation. He is the messenger of the covenant. Concerning this we see that the Holy Spirit is the author of the Word of prophecy contained in the Bible, all of which are applicable to us. We also know that, "all scriptures are given by the inspiration of God" (2 Timothy 3:16)

"We have also a more sure word of prophecy; whereunto ye do well that ye take heed, as unto a light that shineth in a dark place, until the day dawn, and the day star arise in your hearts: -Knowing this first that no prophecy of the scripture is of any private interpretation. For the prophecy came not in old time by the will of man: but holy men of God spake as they were moved by the Holy Ghost." (2 Peter 1:19-21, KJV).

We can conclude that the Holy Spirit is the Author of the Scriptures. Therefore, He is the Number One authority in interpreting and revealing the intention and the heart of the Father God, concerning all of the scriptures. (See Job 33:21-25).

Faith based on Holy-Spirit inspired revelation of the Word is what is effective and applicable to life and living. The Holy Spirit unveils, He makes you see the direction to go, in faith. You cannot doubt what you can see. We have a "more sure Word…"

Meditation is a very important spiritual access to revelation. Meditation is spiritual and mental interaction with the Word of God as contained in the Bible and the Author of the Bible, which is the Holy Spirit.

Through meditation, you ponder, consider, and think about the Word of God, allowing the Holy Spirt to break down the Word, to you personally, for direct application to real life situation. You imagine the Word being relevant to your life, and how to fulfil your own responsibility in this Word.

In meditation, Light comes to you and energise your spirit, soul and even body, to action. As you meditate, you start speaking out loud, mutter and utter the Word. Meditation allows you to also be imparted by the presence of the Lord and to behold Him as you commune with the Spirit of Truth. He reveals and also imparts Truth to you.

Meditation empowers you to do whatever the Word says to do, because in meditation, the Word of God becomes ingrained inside and becomes part of you. The Word becomes deep-seated and deep-rooted inside, and makes you "see" – revelation. You are empowered by the Spirit of the Word.

For example, when you meditate enough on scriptures, as the below, you see yourself fruitful and full of health, and you cannot imagine yourself being barren or sick. Faith is deposited in you.

"Thou shalt be blessed above all people: there shall not be male or female barren among you, or among your cattle. - And the LORD will take away from thee all sickness, and will put none of the evil diseases of Egypt, which thou knowest, upon thee; but will lay them upon all them that hate thee." (Deuteronomy 7:14-15)

Through meditation of the scripture, you are imparted with the Truth of your redemption rights and your inheritance in Christ Jesus, through revelation by the Holy Spirit.

"But as it is written, eye has not seen, nor ear heard, nor have entered into the heart of man, the things which God has prepared for those who love Him. **But God has revealed them to us through His Spirit.** *For the Spirit searches all things, yes, the deep things of God.*

For what man knows the things of a man except the spirit of the man which is in him? Even so no one knows the things of God except the Spirit of God. Now we have received, not the spirit of the world, but the Spirit who is from God, that we might know the things that have been freely given to us by God." (1 Corinthians 2:9-12)

In meditation, your mind is also renewed, which means that, you start to think in line with the Word of God, rather than according to the dictates or expectations of men, or natural circumstances. It is easier to walk by faith when your mind agrees with the Word – the spirit of unbelief, is flushed out. Transformation is inevitable.

"...be ye transformed by the renewal of your mind...." *(Romans 12:2).*

Winning Faith Is Rhema-Provoked Faith

What is *"rhema"*? Rhema is a Greek word for "spoken Word" or "utterance" – that, which is or has been uttered by the living voice. It is as different from the "written Word" or Word in the thought (*logos*).

Rhema-provoked faith, is based on the Voice of the Lord to you concerning the matter of relevance in your life –whether in relation to what you are believing for, your situation, what God wants you to do or just any Divine instruction. It's a specific spoken word of revelation or instruction about what to do. It will be scripturally based, but not necessarily a scriptural verse.

Behind every statement of Scripture is the Voice of the Lord.

The scriptural verse may say one thing and the application of that scripture is generally understood, in context and in wider application. However, the Spirit of the Lord, may speak concerning the same scripture, in relation to a specific issue at hand, in a way that, there is no mistake about the specific application of the scripture. And although, that may not be exactly in context with the scripture, but will be in order, and in context with the life application at that time.

For example, Jesus announced His ministry with the scriptures in Luke 4:18-19, which is a quote from Isaiah 60:1-2. When the Lord called me into the ministry, this scripture came, very strongly in my spirit, as the "Rhema" Word for the ministry. I "saw" that this is what the ministry is ordained to be about.

"The Spirit of the Lord is upon me, because he has anointed me to preach the gospel to the poor; He has sent me to heal the broken-hearted, to proclaim liberty to the captives and recovery of sight to the blind, to set at liberty those who are oppressed; to proclaim the acceptable year of the LORD."

When R*hema* comes, and it is recognised as such, it is a strong foundation for faith. Rhema is un-mistakenly compelling, in a way, that is difficult for others to understand and relate to, unless the Spirit of God, speaks the same R*hema* to them.

"So then faith cometh by hearing, and hearing by the word (Rhema) of God." (Romans 10:17, KJV)

God can thunder revelation or instructions to you through the scriptures or directly to your spirit. The Word or instruction comes with Peace and Joy, but may not necessarily be easy. The voice of the Lord is a joyful sound, and faith will come with it.

"Blessed is the people that know the joyful sound: they shall walk, O LORD, in the light of thy countenance." (Psalms 89:15)

No one can truly hear from God and doubt Him. In the Bible, especially in the Old Testament, it is common to read "And the Voice of the Lord came....saying..." The "voice of the Lord" occurs 45 times in the Bible. "The Lord said" occurs 215 times. "And God said" occurs 29 times. This means that speaking Rhema-Word is an important way that God communicates with us by His Holy Spirit into our spirit.

"The voice of the LORD is upon the waters: the God of glory thundereth: the LORD is upon many waters. The voice of the LORD is powerful; the voice of the LORD is full of majesty." (Psalms 29:3-4)

We must start discerning and responding positively to the Voice of God. Jesus said *"My sheep hear my voice..."* As long as the Voice, does not contradict the Word of God, and neither is the content and context of the Voice, contrary to the Person and the Nature of God, as revealed in the scriptures, it is just as faith-generating and as powerful, as the written Word.

Many of the patriarchs did not have the opportunity or the luxury of the compiled Bible, in the way we have it today. Nonetheless, they took the Word of God and the Voice of the

Spirit seriously, in whichever format they were recorded, whether in the tablets of stone, or in papyrus form.

When God speaks to you, Faith is imparted to take on the challenge.

God's Voice swallows up all doubt. This is the impartation of faith through the Voice of the Lord. Effective, winning or dominion faith must be Rhema-Word based.

"Is not my word like a fire?" says the LORD, *"And like a hammer that breaks the rock in pieces?" (Jeremiah 23:29)*

The Voice of the Lord is powerful and will destroy everything that stands as rock, including every doubt and unbelief. Receive it, now, in Jesus Name!

Winning Faith Is Prompt Action-Based Faith.

Prompt faith is immediate, swift, rapid, quick and ready faith. Prompt, swift, rapid and quick are all action words, either directly or indirectly. Action-based faith or action-driven faith is a winning faith. Any faith that does not show or result in action is fake. God weighs our actions.

"Yea, a man may say, Thou hast faith, and I have works: shew me thy faith without thy works, and I will shew thee my faith by my works." (James 2:18)

"Alexander the coppersmith did me much evil: the Lord reward him according to his works: Of whom be thou ware also; for he hath greatly withstood our words." (2 Timothy 4:14-15)

The Lord weighs our actions and rewards accordingly. Winning faith is a moving, prompt faith. Abraham moved immediately to circumcise his family, on the basis of Divine instruction (Genesis 17). He did this to his whole family "in the self-same day, as God had said to him". What God said was very important to him.

"And Abraham took Ishmael his son, and all that were born in his house, and all that were bought with his money, every male among the men of Abraham's house; and circumcised the flesh of their foreskin in the self-same day, as God had said unto him." (Genesis 17:23)

Abraham departed promptly to go to Mount Moriah to sacrifice Isaac (Genesis 22). God weighs our actions in other to determine our manifestation. Faith that quickly responds to God, is faith that Values God, Honours God and acknowledges the Supremacy of God. There was no time to consider or discuss the pros and cons of what the Lord had told him. It was more important to obey God than to reason, or compromise.

"Then He said, "Take now your son, your only son Isaac, whom you love, and go to the land of Moriah, and offer him there as a burnt offering on one of the mountains of which I

shall tell you." ³ So Abraham rose early in the morning and saddled his donkey, and took two of his young men with him, and Isaac his son; and he split the wood for the burnt offering, and arose and went to the place of which God had told him." (Genesis 22:2-3)

This is the sort of faith that provokes the "sworn blessing" of God: when God swears a blessing over your life, He will see to it that it comes to pass, now and in the generations to come. This is what happened to Abraham, because of His prompt-action faith.

There was no delaying, there was no negotiating, or rationalising. Faith is an act of obedience in God. Abraham had every opportunity to change his mind or reason in contrary to what God was telling him to do, but he refused to compromise, even ready to kill his only son of promise, for the sake of obedience first. Faith is obeying; it is the highest level of trust.

Abraham was convinced that God is so faithful to His Word, so even if his son was killed as a sacrifice, God will still raise him up, in order to fulfil His promise to him, of being biologically, the original father of many nations.

"Then the Angel of the LORD *called to Abraham a second time out of heaven, and said: "By Myself I have sworn, says the* LORD, *because you have done this thing, and have not withheld your son, your only son— blessing I will bless you, and multiplying I will multiply your descendants as the stars*

of the heaven and as the sand which is on the seashore; and your descendants shall possess the gate of their enemies. In your seed all the nations of the earth shall be blessed, because you have obeyed my voice." (Genesis 22:15-18)

Noah also did something similar. He obeyed God, in faith, with prompt action, on what God asked him to do, despite the fact that, it was totally unreasonable, and even mock-provoking amongst his people. He obeyed God, rather than please his friends, family, colleagues or community.

"Thus Noah did; according to all that God commanded him, so he did." (Genesis 6:22)

Noah moved, with reverence. Winning faith is a moving faith. Remember that belated action could be a strong sign of unbelief. Sometimes, as time passes, the impact of a divine instruction becomes less, as it creates doubt and apathy.

"By faith Noah, being warned of God of things not seen as yet, moved with fear, prepared an ark to the saving of his house; by the which he condemned the world, and became heir of the righteousness which is by faith." (Hebrews 11:7, KJV)

Winning Faith is Prompt - High-Level Disciplined Faith.

What is discipline? Discipline is forcing yourself or making yourself do something that is required to be done, despite the fact that, you really do not feel like doing it and/or you don't want to do it – but you do it anyway because, it is necessary or because, it is the right thing to do – to achieve a desired goal or to make something favourable happen.

Without discipline, it is not possible to achieve anything tangible in life. Often the difference between success and failure is the discipline one is ready to apply in the achievement of a goal, or in the path one has chosen or in the pursuit of destiny.

Discipline is at the heart of day to day choices or decisions. The more we are prepared to force ourselves or make ourselves do (whatever) - despite the fact that we really don't feel like doing those things that lead to our lifting, promotion, progress, the more we take charge and are in control of the happenings in our lives.

Faith is a spiritual force governed by spiritual laws and principles. So whether one likes it or not, the demands of faith is not going to change, because of tradition, culture, previous teaching, political correctness or personal preferences.

It is important to accept and settled with the truth that High-level disciplined faith demands; that you think right, speak right, speak of those things which be not, as though they were.

Believe that you have received, do not look at circumstances, be daring, patient and consistent, be thankful and full of praise, and be at rest, without fear, worry or complaining – all these happening simultaneously.

CHAPTER 6

BUT, HOW DO I KNOW I'M IN FAITH?

We have already discussed the seven characteristics of effective or winning faith. During this discussion we identified things that:

- Winning Faith Is Rhema-Provoked Faith
- Winning Faith Is Revelation-Based Faith
- Winning Faith Is Word-Based Faith
- Winning Faith Is Prompt Action-Based Faith
- Winning Faith is Fighting Faith
- Winning Faith is a Daring Faith
- Winning Faith is a High-Level Disciplined Faith

In discussing the importance of ensuring that our faith is highly disciplined, we talked about seven areas that many people get caught out in faith. They allow their faith to bounce off and on or up and down, such that this inconsistency of faith delays the answer, and in some cases, they give up before the answer comes. I want you to be reassured that your faith will produce, if you don't give up. However, you don't want to become tired out, during the waiting period. You also need to be making adjustments, during the waiting period.

The following areas are the common ones that adjustment is necessary. We discussed them before.

Highly disciplined Faith:

- Faith is not Faith, unless it is Speaking Faith
- Faith is not Faith, unless it is Thinking Right.
- Faith is not Faith, unless it in the Now.
- Faith is not Faith, unless it is Patient
- Faith does not look at the Circumstances.
- Faith is not Faith, unless it is joyful, thankful and Praiseful
- Faith Is not Faith, unless it is rested and worry-free faith and fearless

Unbelief rubs us of seeing the Mighty Hand of God in our lives. Faith that is not highly disciplined is still faith and I do sincerely believe on the basis of the Bible describing various levels of faith, (no faith, little faith, great faith and the spirit or gift of faith), that faith that is not as highly disciplined as ticking ALL the "boxes" above, will still get results.

"And he could there do no mighty work, save that he laid his hands upon a few sick folk, and healed them. And he

marvelled because of their unbelief. And he went round about the villages, teaching." (Mark 6:5-6)

They got some results in the environment of unbelief, but not much. Your faith will avail much in Jesus Name.

Are You Really in Faith?

Sometimes it is possible to think that you have ticked all the "faith checklists" and still find that the manifestation is being delayed. The first thing to consider is "am I really in faith"? The second consideration is to ask the question – "what is the Divine Timing about this issue?" and thirdly, "is my faith under trial?"

"Examine yourselves as to whether you are in the faith. Test yourselves. Do you not know yourselves, that Jesus Christ is in you?—unless indeed you are disqualified." (2 Corinthians 13:5)

We are not going to discuss much about the last two: however, if your faith is being tried, and you are walking with the Lord, God will reveal this to you. It will come as an unexplainable reassurance and peace that you should continue to do what you are doing, in steadfastness and patience.

Regarding divine timing, God will lead you. God will speak to you regarding His set time, so that there will be no concerns but peace that will keep your heart and mind in Christ Jesus.

In the final analysis, your faith will produce, just like Abraham. Abraham, was listening to Divine direction and walking with God, to ensure that God's purposes are fulfilled in his life. That is what matters. Trust is hope that has found rest. It will see you through trial of faith.

"My brethren, count it all joy when you fall into various trials, knowing that the testing of your faith produces patience. But let patience have its perfect work, that you may be perfect and complete, lacking nothing." (James 1:2-4)

So how do you know that you are in faith? How can you gauge your faith level? You know whether you are in faith or not, by assessing your dominant thoughts about what you are believing for. You assess whether your constant and dominant thoughts and considerations concerning what you are believing God for are based on the circumstances or based on the Word.

In order words, if what you are constantly and mostly thinking about is what God - The Word- said about your circumstances, then your thoughts are thoughts of faith. If what you are constantly and mostly thinking about is what the circumstances are, and you base your immediate expectation on this, your faith does need to "come up higher."

If your constant dominant thoughts and meditations are about what you are going through, the problem you are facing, how difficult things are, then, you are **not** walking by faith. At best, you are thinking natural thoughts, that's if that is not causing you to worry, and at worst, you are thinking unbelief.

You become what you think about, you give birth to your most dominant thoughts - whether its unbelief, fear or faith – whether it is what you want or what you don't want! As a man thinks in his heart, so is he. This is why it is mandatory - it's an absolute necessity that you have a Word or some specific promise from the Scriptures to guide your thinking, about what you are believing God for.

Therefore, if you find yourself actively thinking more about the problem more than what the Word says, thus getting agitated or worried, about it, then know straight away that, you are **not** in faith. What you think about is what you end up talking about. Because out of the abundance of the heart the mouth speaks. Your words are an integral part of your faith walk.

Your Faith Gauge

We often hear ourselves, ministers or people talk about the level of faith - what is my level of faith? Am I really walking by faith on this issue? The following statement will help you.

The level or the ease at which your thoughts go either to your situation or to the Word of God about your situation, is the level of faith you are currently operating in. This does not mean you do not think about your situation at all.

However, the ease at which you believe what God says, can arrest, dominate, and take hold of your thoughts about the situation, is an indication of your level of faith. If you are constantly shifting between what the natural circumstance is saying to you and what the Word says, it means that the Word of God has not gained dominion over your mind about this issue. There is no rest. Your soul is agitated. You are still double minded. Remember James 1:7-8

"For let not that man suppose that he will receive anything from the Lord; he is a double-minded man, unstable in all his ways."

Remember that, **Faith is full persuasion - absolute agreement with the Word of God - beyond which it is impossible to change or doubt or be convinced otherwise, on any grounds - given time place person or circumstances.**

Faith is not sensible. It is stubborn, and when based on God's Word, working with the Holy Spirit in its operations, it will no doubt produce.

Dealing with Struggling Faith

What do you do, when you find you are not walking in faith or you feel that your faith is struggling (at your level of faith). Rather than coming to a place of absolute confidence - that you believe you already have what you desire?

1. You simply take time out. Put it on your priority list to go to the original scriptures that your faith is based on. If there is no specific scripture, you must find one or some. Ask for help.

2. Spend time to meditate on the scripture(s) or promise(s) about what you are believing for. If possible, write down what you are trusting God for, on a separate piece of paper or preferably a journal, and write down all the scriptures or Word of God that promises you what you are trusting for.

Meditate on them, imagine them coming to pass in your life, and see yourself with the result or answer. Imagine the Word working for you. Imagine the force of faith going about, actively busy, on your project.

3. Start speaking or declaring and affirming what the Word says about the situation. If necessary, do this SEVERAL times a day. You are programming your mind, to agree with the Word of God. You are sowing the seeds of faith into your heart. Faith will come into your heart, as you hear yourself declare the Word of Promise - Romans 10:17.

If you set apart this period of intensive interaction with the Word of God, an instantaneous shift will occur to your level of faith. But you are likely not to be there yet. You have just started, to make a shift in faith.

4. Maintain a practice of meditation, and confession of the particular scripture until, you come to a place where, it is the Word of God that immediately comes to your heart and mind, anytime your thoughts goes to the situation or issue you are believing for.

When you come to the appropriate level of faith, your heart will be at rest; that "it is done" - regardless of the situation. Revelation will flood your heart. You have the answer. Interestingly enough, you are the only one who knows when you reach this place of faith. It is a matter of the heart.

People might be able to gauge from what you are saying - or your faith confessions - or from what you are doing - your faith actions - but the faith in your heart or assurance can only be experienced by you. Active faith speaks. If something is really very important to you, you need to give it priority. Your faith walk is a priority.

CHAPTER 7

THE DOMINION OF FAITH EXPLAINED

Faith has Power, it can create its own territory, or domain. Faith can frame its own world as desired, regardless of the surrounding or prevailing situations. You can create or frame your own "world" by faith. By faith we understand that the worlds were framed by the Word of God, so that those things that are visible are made of that which are not visible. This means that the invisible produced and is still producing the visible.

"By faith we understand that the worlds were framed by the word of God, so that the things which are seen were not made of things which are visible." (Hebrews 11:3)

Bible faith is based on the creative Word, therefore faith is creative. It has the ability to allow and disallow because, without the Word, there was nothing made, which was made. Nothing existed without the Word, so nothing existed without faith. Faith is a major spiritual key for exploit. That is why faith has dominion.

"In the beginning was the Word, and the Word was with God, and the Word was God. He was in the beginning with God. All things were made through Him, and without Him nothing was made that was made. In Him was life, and the life was the light of men. And the light shines in the darkness, and the darkness did not comprehend it." (John 1:1-5)

Dominion is the act, right or power to rule, govern, control and the exercising of sovereign authority. It implies exercise of command, mastery and ownership. Dominion also refers to the territory or sphere subject to influence or control, by a sovereign entity. To control means to exercise restraint or direction over, to hold in check, to curb or limit. Control can also be defined as eliminating or preventing the flourishing or spread of something.

The operation of faith confers dominion at all levels – spiritual, mental, emotional, psychological, physically and materially. We have seen this already in various discussions under the force of faith. The force of faith is the force of dominion.

Faith translates you into the realm of God. A Divine Realm and Spiritual Dimension. From the human realm of operation, to the realm of God's power, which is the realm of dominion. Nothing can control God. Therefore only God and nothing else can "control" the person who walks by faith. Even the devil himself, does not have a right of this nature of control, over the born-again human spirit. That is why the Bible says we have been translated into the kingdom of light, by redemption.

"God has freed us from the power of darkness, and he brought us into the kingdom of his dear Son. "The Son paid for our sins, and in him we have forgiveness." (Colossians 1:13-14).

"Jesus said unto him, if thou can believe, all things are possible to him that believeth." (Mark 9:23).

"And Jesus looking upon them saith, with men it is impossible, but not with God: for with God all things are possible." (Mark 10:27).

This means that faith puts the believers in the realm of possibilities. The realm of God, which is the realm of dominion. Therefore faith is the spiritual engraftment of humanity unto Divinity therefore, empowering humanity to operate in the frequency of the Divine. Whatever is possible for God by faith, is possible to whosoever believes, - as we operate in the power of the Almighty, we become Divine personalities.

When someone is operating with this kind of faith and this supernatural level, faith ceases to just be about believing for God to manifest, faith becomes a way in which we carry God into our situations. When you step in (with God), God steps in, because you are operating in agreement, at the same frequency of heaven in faith. Faith brings Gods hand to bear on the affairs of men.

Remember that you are a child of God. By faith you have God dwelling inside you by the Spirit and you also dwell inside of God. Faith engrafts you, into Divinity, while it is operative. You cannot be a child of God and struggle like a child of man. This is because operating by faith is operating in the realm of the spirit, which is the realm of dominion. We now look at some examples of how the operation of faith translates into and empowers one for dominion over various circumstances of life.

"By faith they passed through the Red Sea as by dry land, whereas the Egyptians, attempting to do so, were drowned." (Hebrews 11:29)

Here we see that, faith will not allow them to be stranded. There is always a way out for faith. The man of faith cannot be cornered. By the exercise of faith, the children of Israel were able to dominate their circumstances, through the release of God's power.

Remember that faith is the spiritual medium through which we tap into the power of the Almighty God. It's the channel that connects us to the flow of the Power of God for a change of situation. If God cannot be cornered, then the person operating in the faith of God or God-kind of faith cannot be cornered. Now, that is Dominion because, you will always be in command.

"By faith Sarah herself also received strength to conceive seed, and she bore a child when she was past the age,

because she judged Him faithful who had promised. Therefore from one man, and him as good as dead, were born as many as the stars of the sky in multitude— innumerable as the sand which is by the seashore." (Hebrews 11:11-12)

Faith overcame the circumstance of long-standing barrenness, which had controlled them for all these while. The conception and birth of Isaac by Sarah is testimony to the fact that, although it took long, while Abraham was growing in faith, eventually, faith released into their hands their heart's desire. They had the last laugh. They overcame – That's' Dominion!

Faith puts you in command. There is no need to be concerned here about arrogance because, you are fully aware that it is because of the virtue of the Holy Spirit and operation by the hand of God that you are in command. God wants Your Dominion. God is committed to your dominion. The Bible says that, it is through faith that we subdue kingdoms.

"Who through faith subdued kingdoms, wrought righteousness, obtained promises, stopped the mouths of lions, quenched the violence of fire, escaped the edge of the sword, out of weakness were made strong, waxed valiant in fight, turned to flight the armies of the aliens. Women received their dead raised to life again: and others were

tortured, not accepting deliverance; that they might obtain a better resurrection" (Hebrews 11:33-35)

"Subdue" is another good relative word for dominate (*active verb*) or dominion (*noun*). So dominion means to exert a superior power over, and keep in permanent subjection. You subdue and keep your subject in the state of surrender, meaning that your enemy and the situation is overpowered by faith and is disabled from further resistance. So, faith causes us to walk in unquestionable dominion and authority and superiority over "kingdoms". Kingdom is a domain, in which something is dominant or where something or someone is in charge, in control or in command.

It is therefore, by faith that we live and do right. It is by faith we obtain promises. It is by faith we stop all oppositions, be it spiritual, emotional, physical or natural. Every violence or attack or sword against us is crushed and brought under control and conquered and brought into permanent subjection, by the force and power of faith. By the operation of faith, we can overpower, terminate, disable and subdue the operations of darkness. That's Dominion!

"Above all, taking the shield of faith with which you will be able to quench all the fiery darts of the wicked one. And take the helmet of salvation, and the sword of the Spirit, which is the word of God" (Ephesians 6:16-17)

The power, strength and courage that flows from the operation of faith is undeniable. We fight on valiantly, in the battle of life and turn to flight, the armies of the aliens or strangers by the power of faith. Faith is a Shield of defence, and because the Word of God – the offensive sword of the Spirit - is released in faith, Faith is also an offensive force.

"For whatever is born of God overcomes the world. And this is the victory that has overcome the world—our faith. Who is he who overcomes the world, but he who believes that Jesus is the Son of God?" (1 John 5:4-5).

That's Dominion! The dominion of faith. There are few areas we must seek to apply the dominion of faith in our lives. Let's look at these next.

All-Round Dominion of Faith.

God's original intention is for man to be in command. From Genesis to Revelation, we can see this purpose of God replayed over and over again. God knows and understands the conditions that will make this possible, because at the end of the day, He is the Creator and the Supplier of the Power for dominion.

"And God said, Let us make man in our image, after our likeness: and let them have dominion over the fish of the sea, and over the fowl of the air, and over the cattle, and over all the earth, and over every creeping thing that creepeth upon

the earth. -So God created man in his own image, in the image of God created he him; male and female created he them. And God blessed them, and God said unto them, be fruitful, and multiply, and replenish the earth, and subdue it: and have dominion over the fish of the sea, and over the fowl of the air, and over every living thing that moveth upon the earth." (Genesis 1:26-28)

It is not possible to truly dominate without God. We owe our very existence to God. If the air in the atmosphere were to become all drained out, such that the whole earth becomes a vacuum, man with all its fanciful invention and "civilisation" will not survive twenty-four hours.

The man himself will not survive past five minutes without the need for survival assistance. That is why humanity is forever connected and dependent on the goodwill of God.

All that God has always required is that humanity recognises and acknowledges that He is the Almighty, and this should necessarily result in a permeant state of worship and gratitude to the Creator God. Several times that God has shown His displeasure to mankind, it has always been related to the fact that, man has or is attempting to abdicate his throne of dominion, by being subject to and dominated by the things he created rather than being subject to the Creator God Himself. God is committed to your dominion.

Faith is what accesses this goodwill and power that God has given men. Obedience for example is a manifestation of faith and love. God's will is for your dominion at all levels of existence and engagement of life. Even after life, death is supposed to translate you to another place of dominion, which is Heaven. It is not God's primary intention that any human should go to hell. Hell is designed for fallen spirits.

"The Lord is not slack concerning His promise, as some count slackness, but is longsuffering toward us not willing that any should perish but that all should come to repentance." (2 Peter 3:9)

God is indeed committed to our all-round, eternal dominion! This is an entirely different topic. The essence of this section is to emphasise that, it is the operation of faith that releases us into that all-level, all-round dominion.

So we will just look at a few examples of the dominion of faith in operation.

Dominion of Faith over the Forces of Darkness

The believer has authority and therefore can operate in dominion in the spiritual world, by the reason of redemption. Christ has redeemed us, delivering us from the kingdom of darkness and has positioned us into the kingdom of God – the Kingdom of Light. (Colossians 1:12-14).

Jesus is the Light of the world. Darkness cannot stand light. But darkness is more of the absence of light, rather than the fact that darkness has power of itself. When light refuses to shine, darkness results.

Think about what happens with the Sun and the Moon, or day and night. Christians have given too much credit to the power of darkness and have belittled the power of light!

"Then Jesus spoke to them again, saying, I am the light of the world. He who follows me shall not walk in darkness, but have the light of life." (John 8:12) **"And** *As long as I am in the world, I am the light of the world." (John 9:5)*

Jesus is no longer physically present in the world, as Jesus the Christ.

However He is still present, as we are now the representatives of Jesus. As representatives, agents or ambassadors of the Kingdom, we are empowered and we have the same rights confirmed to us. That is why Jesus also called us light and salt of the world.

"Ye are the salt of the earth: but if the salt have lost his savour, wherewith shall it be salted? it is thenceforth good for nothing, but to be cast out, and to be trodden under foot of men. Ye are the light of the world. A city that is set on a hill cannot be hid. Neither do men light a candle and put it under a bushel, but on a candlestick; and it giveth light unto all that are in the house. Let your light so shine before men,

that they may see your good works, and glorify your Father which is in heaven." (Matthew 5:13-16)

Jesus said, "Let your light shine…" He knows too well that when the light of the believer – the person who has faith in Christ is shining, darkness must withdraw. The Word of God is light and the light cannot be overcome or arrested by darkness. It is impossible. This is the dominion of light over darkness.

"The Word gave life to everything that was created, and his life brought light to everyone. The light shines in the darkness, and the darkness can never extinguish it." (John 1:4-5, NLT).

The New Century Version of verse 5 says – *"The Light shines in the darkness, and the darkness has not overpowered it."*

Darkness cannot overpower light. This means light has eternal dominion over darkness. When the believer stands in faith, as light in this world, and exercise the right of the Kingdom, darkness cannot stand. Jesus demonstrates this very well in His earthly ministry in gospel according to Saint Matthew, chapter 15.

"Then Jesus went out from there and departed to the region of Tyre and Sidon. And behold, a woman of Canaan came from that region and cried out to Him, saying, "Have mercy on me, O Lord, Son of David! My daughter is severely demon-possessed." But He answered her not a word. And His disciples came and urged Him, saying, "Send her away, for

she cries out after us." But He answered and said, "I was not sent except to the lost sheep of the house of Israel." Then she came and worshiped Him, saying, "Lord, help me!"

"But He answered and said, "It is not good to take the children's bread and throw it to the little dogs." And she said, "Yes, Lord, yet even the little dogs eat the crumbs which fall from their masters' table." Then Jesus answered and said to her, "O woman, great is your faith! Let it be to you as you desire." And her daughter was healed from that very hour."

Here, we see clearly the dominion of faith over severe demon possession. We have related this scripture, regarding how the force of faith, can qualify to receive that which is not normally your entitlement - but nevertheless, required for life. The lady here from Tyre and Sidon, was not a Jew. Her daughter who was severely demon-possessed. The daughter was not even present where Jesus was. She operated in faith, regarding the Power of God in Jesus to be released to cast out and dispossess her daughter of demonic occupation.

The operation of faith, released the power of God on her behalf and caused her and her daughter to overpower the forces of darkness in their lives. There is no doubt that she was suffering together with her daughter in the hands of this evil forces, because of the visible effect on her daughter's life.

The Bible says, the result was immediate, despite the fact that there was physical distance between where she and Jesus were and where her daughter was. The dominion of faith knows no distance, because it is a spiritual force. Praise God! So, when he was about to go to heaven, he gave the commission which included the dominion over the powers of darkness.

"And he said unto them, Go ye into all the world, and preach the gospel to every creature. He that believeth and is baptized shall be saved; but he that believeth not shall be damned. These signs shall follow them that believe; in my name shall they cast out devils; they shall speak with new tongues; - They shall take up serpents; and if they drink any deadly thing, it shall not hurt them; they shall lay hands on the sick, and they shall recover. And they went forth, and preached everywhere, the Lord working with them, and confirming the word with signs following. Amen." (Mark 16:15-18, 20).

Like the Gentile woman, faith is the access to everything that we have in Christ. Every spiritual blessing that we have in Christ Jesus are all expressions of the Grace of God.

"Therefore, having been justified by faith, we have peace with God through our Lord Jesus Christ, [2] through whom also we have access by faith into this grace in which we stand, and rejoice in hope of the glory of God." (Romans 5:1-2)

Also, by redemption of Christ, we are now seated in a higher spiritual, heavenly place in Christ - far above, level. This is where we should be operating from, in the realm of the spirit.

"But God, who is rich in mercy, for his great love wherewith he loved us, Even when we were dead in sins, hath quickened us together with Christ, (by grace ye are saved;) And hath raised us up together, and made us sit together in heavenly places in Christ Jesus" (Ephesians 2:4-6)

The Apostle Paul was praying for spiritual understanding and illumination of the believers in Ephesus that they will grasp this truth, because it can sometimes be difficult to believe that a Christian indeed, has so much power in God.

"Therefore I also, after I heard of your faith in the Lord Jesus and your love for all the saints, do not cease to give thanks for you, making mention of you in my prayers: that the God of our Lord Jesus Christ, the Father of glory, may give to you the spirit of wisdom and revelation in the knowledge of Him, the eyes of your understanding being enlightened; that you may know what is the hope of His calling, what are the riches of the glory of His inheritance in the saints, and what is the exceeding greatness of His power toward us who believe, according to the working of His mighty power,

Which He worked in Christ when He raised Him from the dead and seated Him at His right hand in the heavenly places, far above all principality and power and might and dominion, and every name that is named, not only in this age but also in that which is to come. And He put all things under His feet, and gave Him to be head over all things to the church, which is His body, the fullness of Him who fills all in all. (Ephesians 1:15-23)

Lastly, the power to resist the devil steadfastly in faith, until he surrenders and flees, has been given to you. Use it. This is the exercise of your dominion by faith. The requirement is that you humble yourself, and be fearless, not worrying and be bold to exercise your right and privileges in Christ, over the forces of darkness and all they represent.

"Humble yourselves therefore under the mighty hand of God, that he may exalt you in due time: Casting all your care upon him; for he careth for you. Be sober, be vigilant; because your adversary the devil, as a roaring lion, walketh about, seeking whom he may devour: Whom resist stedfast in the faith, knowing that the same afflictions are accomplished in your brethren that are in the world." (1 Peter 5:6-9, KJV).

There is no reason why a Christian believer should be afraid of the forces of darkness. Understanding your identity in Christ and mixing it with faith will cause you to operate in dominion over the forces of darkness.

"Behold, I give unto you power to tread on serpents and scorpions, and over all the power of the enemy: and nothing shall by any means hurt you. Notwithstanding in this rejoice

not, that the spirits are subject unto you; but rather rejoice, because your names are written in heaven." (Luke 10:19-20)

Dominion over Failure

"Ye have not chosen me, but I have chosen you, and ordained you, that ye should go and bring forth fruit, and that your fruit should remain: that whatsoever ye shall ask of the Father in my name, he may give it you." (John 15:16)

Failure is not the perfect will of God for His people. He gave us the necessary recipe for success in His Word. As believers, we are blessed, and cannot be cursed. However life presents us with what amount to blessings, and what could amount to curses, life or death. God encourages us to choose life and choose the blessing.

"For this commandment which I command you today is not too mysterious for you, nor is it far off. It is not in heaven, that you should say, 'Who will ascend into heaven for us and bring it to us that we may hear it and do it?' 'Nor is it beyond the sea, that you should say, 'Who will go over the sea for us and bring it to us that we may hear it and do it?' But the word is very near you, in your mouth and in your heart, that you may do it.

"See, I have set before you today life and good, death and evil, in that I command you today to love the L<small>ORD</small> *your God, to walk in His ways, and to keep His commandments, His*

statutes, and His judgments, that you may live and multiply; and the LORD your God will bless you in the land which you go to possess. I call heaven and earth as witnesses today against you, that I have set before you life and death, blessing and cursing; therefore choose life, that both you and your descendants may live" (Deuteronomy 30:11-16, 19)

How does faith connect us to our dominion over failure? We can see here that, faith is expressed simply by obedience to an instruction given by God. God gave Joshua the recipe for success. Essentially what God was saying is – I am the One who will cause you to be successful.

In the original intention of God for Man, failure is not part of the destiny of Man. We can see that, it is the disobedience in the Garden of Eden that brought the curses, which empowers Man to fail, because he no longer has the backing of God, and all the forces that ensures and guarantees his success are no longer operative in his life. That is why obedience is the key to success, while disobedience is the road that leads to failure.

"This Book of the Law shall not depart from your mouth, but you shall meditate in it day and night, that you may observe to do according to all that is written in it. For then you will make your way prosperous, and then you will have good success." (Joshua 1:8)

The direct connection to this dominion of faith is when Jesus asked Peter to allow Him to use his boat, to preach.

Peter and his business colleagues had just hit a moment of failure. They had spent the whole night at sea, and being in the fishing business, they had blatantly failed.

In this moment of failure, they met Jesus and after Jesus had finished preaching. He gave Peter an instruction, which would lead to an overturn of his failure to success. Peter's obedience in faith, was the link to his dominion over business failure in this instance.

"When He had stopped speaking, He said to Simon, "Launch out into the deep and let down your nets for a catch." But Simon answered and said to Him, "Master, we have toiled all night and caught nothing; nevertheless at your word I will let down the net." And when they had done this, they caught a great number of fish, and their net was breaking. So they signalled to their partners in the other boat to come and help them. And they came and filled both the boats, so that they began to sink." (Luke 5:4-7)

It is important to note that, Peter explained the faith component of this miraculous turn around, which re-established his dominion in the fishing business, even though he then did not continue to follow this line of trade permanently. He said;

"...Master, we have toiled all night and caught nothing, nevertheless at your word I will let down the net."

Jesus asked Peter to follow Him, as He will make him the fisher of men. I passionately believe that it was the operation of faith that turned failure into success.

In the same way, this dominion of faith can be experienced in our lives, as we learn to obey instructions rather than depend on our natural or professional expertise, in the world of commerce, ministry or business.

Dominion over Sickness and Diseases

"How God anointed Jesus of Nazareth with the Holy Ghost and with power: who went about doing good, and healing all that were oppressed of the devil; for God was with him." (Acts 10:38)

The will of God for us is health, wholeness, vitality and healing, when required. This aspect of God is so important that God revealed Himself to mankind as Jehovah Shalom and Jehovah Raphe. The God of Peace and wholeness - with nothing missing and nothing broken and the God that healeth thee. (The operation of faith establishes your dominion over sickness and diseases).

"Now when Jesus had entered Capernaum, a centurion came to Him, pleading with Him, saying, "Lord, my servant is lying at home paralyzed, dreadfully tormented." And Jesus said to him, "I will come and heal him."

The centurion answered and said, "Lord, I am not worthy that you should come under my roof. But only speak a word, and my servant will be healed. For I also am a man under authority, having soldiers under me. And I say to this one, 'Go,' and he goes; and to another, 'Come,' and he comes; and to my servant, 'Do this,' and he does it." When Jesus heard it, He marvelled, and said to those who followed, "Assuredly, I say to you, I have not found such great faith, not even in Israel!" (Matthew 8:5-10)

The force of faith established the dominion of the centurion over the sickness and disease being suffered by his servant. Faith is the power that God has released in the hand of His people, to allow Him to act on our behalf.

Healing is children's bread. And it is the force of faith that allows us to partake of this inherence of the saints.

"Giving thanks to the Father who has qualified us to be partakers of the inheritance of the saints in the light." (Colossians 1:12)

When Jesus made public declaration of His earthly ministry, it is clear that He revealed the heart of the father concerning His desire for His people to experience dominion over sickness and diseases and poverty and distresses.

"The Spirit of the LORD is upon me, because He has anointed me to preach the gospel to the poor; He has sent me to heal the broken hearted, to proclaim liberty to the captives and

recovery of sight to the blind, to set at liberty those who are oppressed" (Luke 4:18)

Dominion over nature and forces of nature

Man has demonstrated dominion over the creations of God, in form of dominion over plants and animal and some natural forces, like damming of the rivers, manipulating the plant and animal kingdom in form through molecular science and genetic modifications. This is consistent with Genesis 1:28, which we have mentioned before:

"Then God blessed them, and God said to them, "Be fruitful and multiply; fill the earth and subdue it; have dominion over the fish of the sea, over the birds of the air, and over every living thing that moves on the earth."

Nonetheless, there is another higher level of dominion that Jesus experienced, demonstrated and then gave us access to, by the operation of faith. Jesus spoke to a tree, walked on water and after His death, walked through wall and ascended to heaven, overcoming the law of gravity.

The raising of the dead recorded in His ministry meant that natural laws and forces of nature had to be put aside, by the operation of faith. Faith indeed is the believer's access to the world of dominion.

"So Jesus said to them, "Because of your unbelief; for assuredly, I say to you, if you have faith as a mustard seed,

you will say to this mountain, 'Move from here to there,' and it will move; and nothing will be impossible for you" (Matthew 17:20)

Jesus spoke to the wind, rebuking it, keeping it in subjection to the dominion of faith, as He also rebuked the disciples, for their fear and lack of faith. Jesus also walked on water and when Peter tried to do the same, he succeeded, as long as he did not allow doubt to overcome his mind, because of what he could see. This is a manifestation of high level dominion faith.

"Immediately Jesus made His disciples get into the boat and go before Him to the other side, while He sent the multitudes away. And when He had sent the multitudes away, He went up on the mountain by Himself to pray. Now when evening came, He was alone there. But the boat was now in the middle of the sea, tossed by the waves, for the wind was contrary.

"Now in the fourth watch of the night Jesus went to them, walking on the sea. And when the disciples saw Him walking on the sea, they were troubled, saying, "It is a ghost!" And they cried out for fear. But immediately Jesus spoke to them, saying, "Be of good cheer! It is I; do not be afraid." And Peter answered Him and said, "Lord, if it is you, command me to come to you on the water." So He said, "Come." And when Peter had come down out of the boat, he walked on the water to go to Jesus.

But when he saw that the wind was boisterous, he was afraid; and beginning to sink he cried out, saying, "Lord, save me!" And immediately Jesus stretched out His hand and caught him, and said to him, "O you of little faith, why did you doubt?" **32** *And when they got into the boat, the wind ceased." (Matthew 14:22-31)*

Dominion of Faith over Poverty and Lack

Poverty and lack is rife amongst mankind and the believers are not immune, unless they know how to walk in the dominion of faith in this area. There is more to this topic than can be discussed in the context of this book, but the bottom line is God wants His people to prosper and have enough and more than enough, and this is possible through obedience to the Word of faith concerning provision.

God established and revealed Himself as the El-Shaddai – the God who is more than enough and Jehovah Jireh – who is the supernatural provider for His people. The very nature of God is opposed to His people suffering because of poverty.

However, as we see, the choices that we make and our disobedience to the laws of faith and laws of abundance causes us to experience much less than God's provision. It is time to rise up and step into faith and learn how to permanently destroy the spirit of poverty in our lives. Jesus said:

"I am the door. If anyone enters by me, he will be saved, and will go in and out and find pasture. The thief does not come except to steal, and to kill, and to destroy. I have come that they may have life, and that they may have it more abundantly." (John 10:9-10)

As the good shepherd, He expressed His will for His sheep, to go in and out to find pasture. Pasture here refers to food and feeding and provision, which is one of the main things the shepherd does for the sheep. Once you understand this, you can easily connect with the fact that, Jesus fed the people supernaturally, when there was nothing physically available for them to eat. He is the manna that comes from heaven for the children of Israel. That is why He said, man shall not live or have his sustenance by bread alone, but by every Word that proceed from the mouth of God.

It means that, if you have the Word of faith, you can live by that because, the dominion of faith will overcome lack and provide for you, even supernaturally, if required.

To explain the need to release faith in the provision of bread – or sustenance, he rebuked his disciples and commented on their "little faith", because it appeared they were causing a stir amongst themselves, because they thought Jesus was talking about natural bread, therefore worrying about how they were going to find bread, at that moment. This is similar to the mind-set of worry about food, and clothes that He rebuked them about in Matthew 6:25-34.

"Now when His disciples had come to the other side, they had forgotten to take bread. Then Jesus said to them, "Take heed and beware of the leaven of the Pharisees and the Sadducees." And they reasoned among themselves, saying, "It is because we have taken no bread."

But Jesus, being aware of it, said to them, "O you of little faith, why do you reason among yourselves because you have brought no bread? Do you not yet understand, or remember the five loaves of the five thousand and how many baskets you took up? Nor the seven loaves of the four thousand and how many large baskets you took up?" (Matthew 16:5-10)

The redemption of believer from the curses of the law, which includes sickness, disease, poverty and death is very much an established new covenant right.

"Christ has redeemed us from the curse of the law, having become a curse for us (for it is written, "Cursed is everyone who hangs on a tree"), that the blessing of Abraham might come upon the Gentiles in Christ Jesus, that we might receive the promise of the Spirit through faith." (Galatian 3:13-14)

The truth is that, the believer today, despite not being of natural Jewish origin, has access to the promises of the blessing of Abraham, which is accessed by faith. That the blessing of Abraham might come on the Gentiles, through faith clearly establishes the dominion of faith over sickness, diseases, poverty, lack and any other know or unknown curses of the law.

"Therefore know that only those who are of faith are sons of Abraham. And the Scripture, foreseeing that God would justify the Gentiles by faith, preached the gospel to Abraham beforehand, saying, "In you all the nations shall be blessed."¹ So then those who are of faith are blessed with believing Abraham." (Galatians 3:7-9)

We are indeed children of promise, in the same way Isaac was the child of promise to Abraham. Faith is what gives us this undeniable access through Jesus Christ to the inheritance.

"For you are all sons of God through faith in Christ Jesus. For as many of you as were baptized into Christ have put on Christ. There is neither Jew nor Greek, there is neither slave nor free, there is neither male nor female; for you are all one in Christ Jesus.

And if you are Christ's, then you are Abraham's seed, and heirs according to the promise." (Galatians 3: 26-29)

"Now we, brethren, as Isaac was, are children of promise." (Galatians 4:28)

That must be the reason why the Apostle Paul prayed the prayer that gave us an insight into the heart of the father, about our all-round – spirit, soul and body prosperity and therefore dominion.

"Beloved, I pray that you may prosper in all things and be in health, just as your soul prospers." (3 John 2)

The operation of faith indeed has dominion over poverty and lack. The blessing is clearly stated in Deuteronomy, and it is clearly intended to the child of God in a place of dominion. He said, "…you shall be the head and not the tail, above only and not beneath." That is your portion.

CHAPTER 8

FAITH BOOSTERS – FAITH COMPANIONS

"Faith Boosters" are things that enhance, facilitate, promotes and supports the operation of faith, so that faith can produce the desired results. Faith rarely works in isolation. Faith is always in context. That is why it is sometimes quite difficult to understand, why someone, who apparently looks like a man or woman of faith struggles to receive answers, than another one, who appears to have little faith.

Faith is a virtue of the Spirit. Therefore anything that affect the spirit will affect faith. Anything that boosts the spirit-life will also boost faith. Here we would only consider five of the Faith Boosters:

- Love
- Prayer (with Fasting)
- Kingdom Service
- Intimacy With God (Personal Walk, Spiritual Maturity)

- Praying in the Tongues

Faith Works By love

Faith and love cannot work by themselves alone: faith works by love and love also works by faith. Love cannot flourish where faith does not thrive. The faith that is productive is activated by love and the love that will be fruitful must be rooted in faith. Faith is a walk! We walk by the truth, not by sight –that is, not by facts.

We walk by revelation, not by sight or circumstances. Whatever affects our Christian walk will also affect our faith walk. **Love that affects Faith is three-dimensional. There is the love of God, the Love for God and the Love for others.**

The Bible says that Faith works by Love. It is expressly stated in Galatians (5:6, KJV).

"For in Jesus Christ neither circumcision availeth anything, nor uncircumcision; but faith which worketh by love."

"For in Christ Jesus neither circumcision nor uncircumcision avails anything, but faith working through love." (Galatians 5:6)

"When we are in Christ Jesus, it is not important if we are circumcised or not. The important thing is faith—the kind of faith that works through love."

We can say therefore that faith towards God works by these three dimensional love. Here the apostle Paul, by the Holy Spirit made this statement in context of discussion about circumcision.

Although this verse talks more about faith for salvation and righteousness and righteous-living, it can be applied to faith for or faith in other things of God, because faith is the same in the Kingdom of God, whatever the context. Here we see that faith works, not because of any natural achievement, but simply because, God loves us, we love God and because we love God, we must love His people.

"If someone says, "I love God," and hates his brother, he is a liar; for he who does not love his brother whom he has seen, how can[c] he love God whom he has not seen?" (1 John 4:20).

Now a lot of teachings that I have received talks more about faith works, because we love others. Yes this is true on the basis of the scriptures above. Faith works as we live in love towards other people. However, this verse also refers to the other two dimensions of love.

Faith works, because God loves us and because we love God. Let me explain further. The love of God is the fundamental reason why He does things for us. There is no greater love than to give your only Son:

"For God so loved the world that He gave His only begotten Son, that whoever believes in Him should not perish but have everlasting life. For God did not send His Son into the world

to condemn the world, but that the world through Him might be saved." (John 3:16-17)

Our ability to see this God, who loves us so much to give His best to us, inspires and fires our faith because we know that, according to Romans, if He loves us so much, by giving His best, there is nothing else that He cannot give us. So we entrust our lives to Him and release our faith in His love for us.

"What then shall we say to these things? If God is for us, who can be against us? He who did not spare His own Son, but delivered Him up for us all, how shall He not with Him also freely give us all things?" (Romans 8:31-32).

This is really very comforting and at the same time faith-boosting - It boosts our faith to be reassured of His unconditional love for us. Let's look at another translation, for clarity:

"So, what do you think? With God on our side like this, how can we lose? If God didn't hesitate to put everything on the line for us, embracing our condition and exposing himself to the worst by sending his own Son, is there anything else he wouldn't gladly and freely do for us?" (Romans 8:31-32, MSG)

It is also true that our love for Him boosts are faith. The more you love someone, the more you can trust them – either to do things for you or to rely on them to keep a secret or to have your interest at heart. If they tell you things, it's easier to believe the words of someone you love, than someone you don't. Similarly, our love and passion for God and the things of God, spills over into our trusting Him.

Lastly, love is a command. Loving God is obeying His command to love others.

"If you love me, keep my commandments." (John 14:15)

"This is my commandment, that you love one another as I have loved you. Greater love has no one than this, than to lay down one's life for his friends." (John 15:12-13)

As we have seen in 1 John 4:20, if we do not love others, especially the people of God, that we have seen, how can we say we love God that we have not seen. Our love for God is also manifested in our love for others!

To make this practical, please understand that love is a fruit of the spirit which must be resident, which is an ingredient which must be visible in every believer. Lack of love will hinder the work of faith. 1 Corinthian 13:4-8, describe the love we are talking about in practical terms. The Love of God, love for God and the love for others, is the same as this "Agape" love.

This is why we need to talk about un-forgiveness, because forgiveness is an expression of love and it enhances faith, while un-forgiveness will hinder faith. A heart-free from un-forgiveness, offenses and, bitterness, can operate in faith much easier than a heart that is filled with such negative emotions. Love does not serve only those who deserve it. Love does not serve only those who can repay it. Love does it for God, who must be seen in awe, through the eyes of faith.

Do allow the piece I wrote below, in one of our newsletters to encourage your walk of obedience in faith for forgiveness.

Is Un-forgiveness Stopping Your Flow of Blessing?

Permit me to share these scriptures by reproducing them entirely as Jesus taught. Is un-forgiveness blocking your blessing? Is it blocking your prosperity? I met an individual recently, who is under severe bondage, of all sorts - spiritual, emotional, financial, physical etc. The moment I mentioned "Forgiveness", it was like something ugly rose up inside - I have touched a very raw and sore wound of the heart..... Un-forgiveness is like cancer, don't let it eat you up, it might be rather too late.

Do this simple test - if you see or think about someone, or something - and immediately fills you with disgust, disapproval, sadness, anger, feeling of revenge or even fear - you are likely to be harbouring un-forgiveness in your heart toward them. You are Free in Jesus Name.

"Then Peter came to him and asked, "Lord, how often should I forgive someone who sins against me? Seven times?" "No, not seven times," Jesus replied, "but seventy times seven! "Therefore, the Kingdom of Heaven can be compared to a

king who decided to bring his accounts up to date with servants who had borrowed money from him. In the process, one of his debtors was brought in who owed him millions of dollars. He couldn't pay, so his master ordered that he be sold—along with his wife, his children, and everything he owned—to pay the debt. "But the man fell down before his master and begged him, 'Please, be patient with me, and I will pay it all.' Then his master was filled with pity for him, and he released him and forgave his debt. (Matthew 18:21-27, NLT)

"But when the man left the king, he went to a fellow servant who owed him a few thousand dollars. He grabbed him by the throat and demanded instant payment. "His fellow servant fell down before him and begged for a little more time. 'Be patient with me, and I will pay it,' he pleaded.

But his creditor wouldn't wait. He had the man arrested and put in prison until the debt could be paid in full. "When some of the other servants saw this, they were very upset. They went to the king and told him everything that had happened. Then the king called in the man he had forgiven and said, 'you evil servant! I forgave you that tremendous debt because you pleaded with me.

Shouldn't you have mercy on your fellow servant, just as I had mercy on you?' Then the angry king sent the man to prison to be tortured until he had paid his entire debt. "That's what my heavenly Father will do to you if you refuse to forgive your brothers and sisters from your heart." (Matthew 18:28-35 NLT)

Pray from your heart - Lord, I release everyone - name them - who have hurt or done me wrong - consciously or unconsciously - NOW, by the Power of Your Holy Spirit, in Jesus Name. I am free, I am free. The pipeline of God's grace and blessing is reopened in my life. (Amen)

Prayer with Fasting Boosts Faith

There is a very popular verse of the Bible, where Jesus made a statement, that "if you can believe, or preferably, if you have faith – all things are possible to him that believes or has faith". We often refer to this scripture outside of context. While this is not wrong, the truth that faith works by prayer, can be explained by this event, which happened in the ministry of Jesus.

"And when He came to the disciples, He saw a great multitude around them, and scribes disputing with them. Immediately, when they saw Him, all the people were greatly amazed, and running to Him, greeted Him. And He asked the scribes, "What are you discussing with them?" Then one of the crowd answered and said, "Teacher, I brought you my son, who has a mute spirit.

And wherever it seizes him, it throws him down; he foams at the mouth, gnashes his teeth, and becomes rigid. So I spoke to your disciples that they should cast it out, but they could not." He answered him and said, "O faithless generation, how long shall I be with you? How long shall I bear with you? Bring him to me." Then they brought him to Him.

And when he saw Him, immediately the spirit convulsed him, and he fell on the ground and wallowed, foaming at the mouth. So He asked his father, "How long has this been happening to him?"

And he said, "From childhood. And often he has thrown him both into the fire and into the water to destroy him. But if you can do anything, have compassion on us and help us." Jesus said to him, "If you can believe, all things are possible to him who believes." immediately the father of the child cried out and said with tears, "Lord, I believe; help my unbelief!" (Mark 9:14-24)

Here we see, that when the disciples with the people with them related the issue of difficulty of ministering healing to the boy that was dumb and epileptic to Jesus – the first thing he said – was "O faithless generation, how long shall I be with you ...). In essence, he was saying, "how long shall I be with you, to be operating in faith, on your behalf...?" He then told the boy's father – if you can believe... that is if you release your faith... all things are possible to those who release their faith!

In response to Jesus statement, the man poured out in prayer to Jesus – Lord, I have faith, but it is not sufficient for this, help my balance of faith, by supplying your faith, to displace my unbelief or lack of faith. This man, was in prayer mode, in his heart towards Jesus. Jesus saw his sincerity, and responded, to cast out the tormenting spirit by His faith, authority and anointing:

"When Jesus saw that the people came running together, He rebuked the unclean spirit, saying to it: "Deaf and dumb spirit, I command you, come out of him and enter him no more!" Then the spirit cried out, convulsed him greatly, and came out of him. And he became as one dead, so that many said, "He is dead." But Jesus took him by the hand and lifted him up, and he arose." (Mark 9:25-27)

Now, when the disciples arrived home with Jesus, they asked further question, regarding the scenario that they witnessed earlier, and Jesus again, gave us further insight, into how prayer with fasting enhances the operation of faith.

"And when He had come into the house, His disciples asked Him privately, "Why could we not cast it out?" So He said to them, "This kind can come out by nothing but prayer and fasting." (Mark 9:28-29)

Jesus had earlier operated in faith to cast out the deaf and dumb spirit and effected the healing of the boy from convulsing epilepsy. Then, He explained, that moreover, aside the obvious, release of faith, this type of issue only responds to prayer and fasting.

He did not undermine the effect of faith, but here he was intimating the disciples, that His faith, confidence and authority needed to deal with the issue, was enhance by His prior prayer and fasting, otherwise – the healing and deliverance would not have been possible. Prayer (with fasting) enhances our operation of faith. The altar of prayer is the altar of empowerment.

Kingdom Service Boosts Faith

The Kingdom of God is a real kingdom, not an imaginary one, although the Kingdom of God as got the unseen or spiritual component. Every Kingdom is established for a reason and there are rules and regulations, laws and principles that make the Kingdom work to fulfil its purposes.

The Kingdom of God traverses the visible earth and the other planetary systems and the invisible heavens, where heavenly beings do dwell. For the believer, the Kingdom of God and the agenda of this Kingdom is important. It is not to be ignored. This is because the believer is an integral part of the Kingdom. Jesus said:

*"But seek first the **kingdom of God** and His righteousness, and all these things shall be added to you." (Matthew 6:33)*

Jesus differentiated one of the fundamental principles of the Kingdom, in Matthew 6:25-34: when he was discussing with His disciples about Kingdom mind-set to daily living and daily provisions. He explained that people outside of the Kingdom worry, fret and have anxieties about life, what they are going to eat, drink, and wear and other survival issues.

He encouraged those in the Kingdom not to have the same disposition or mind-set about life. He then went on to give an insight into the underlying reasons for worry and anxiety about life. He referred to them as *"O ye of little faith…"*

It takes faith to enjoy the benefits of the Kingdom. It takes faith to live Kingdom lifestyle. Kingdom service is taking an interest in the matters of interest to the Kingdom. There is a basic level of faith that is required to come into the Kingdom.

This is imparted with the Word of Faith at salvation (Romans 10:8-17). As the believer begins and continues to serve, he or she soon start to learn about the application of faith in other areas – not just for the self, selfish or material things. For example, believing God and releasing faith, for the work of God to progress, for the Spirit of God to manifest in a meeting, for a service unit to function effectively, for optimal delivery of Kingdom assignments and so on and so forth.

Engaging in these Kingdom activities, are opportunities to exercise ones faith, in non-selfish ways, but they are exercises in faith, nonetheless. Kingdom service also requires that the believer presses on in the things of the spirit, become knowledgeable about the laws of the Kingdom, and allow opportunities for mentoring and impartations – such as impartation of the spirit of faith. It is like being an apprentice of the Faith Walk. Kingdom service is a training ground for the walk of faith.

"I always thank my God when I mention you in my prayers, because I hear about the love you have for all God's holy people and the faith you have in the Lord Jesus. I pray that the faith you share may make you understand every blessing we have in Christ. I have great joy and comfort, my brother, because the love you have shown to God's people has refreshed them. (Philemon 1:4-7, NCV).

The environment of Kingdom service is an environment of faith and it's bound to expedite growth in the things of God, including the virtue of faith. There is another dimension to serving God and the interest of the Kingdom of God.

"And ye shall serve the LORD your God, and he shall bless thy bread, and thy water; and I will take sickness away from the midst of thee. There shall nothing cast their young, nor be barren, in thy land: the number of thy days I will fulfil." (Exodus 23:25-26)

God looks after the interest of the servant of God. As the believer sees the benefit of serving God and experiences the hand of God upon his or her life, it encourages him or her to trust God more and for bigger things, both spiritual and material. If a believer is not experiencing the hand of God, his or her joy will not be full. If they are asking and receiving, there is fullness of joy. With this comes the confidence of faith:

"Until now you have asked nothing in my name. Ask, and you will receive, that your joy may be full." (John 16:24)

Serving God releases favour towards you and when you operate by faith nonetheless the blessing and favour of God that you experience helps to boost your faith.

"It is sad not to get what you hoped for. But wishes that come true are like eating fruit from the tree of life." (Proverbs 13:12)

A sad person will find it difficult to operate in dominion faith. Their hope and confidence is likely to be cast away (Hebrews 10:35-38), therefore they cannot get the reward of faith. When you serve God and he blesses your bread and your water, and takes sickness away from you and cause you to be a productive and fruitful person, it boosts your faith.

Intimacy with God Boosts Faith

Your personal walk or intimacy with God, is what empowers your spiritual maturity and holy living. God is a Spirit and they that worship Him must worship Him in spirit and in truth (John 4:24). It is possible to have a close, intimate personal relationship with God, according to James 4:7, because God will draw near unto those who draw near to Him.

When you draw near to Him, there is a type and level of spiritual experience and impartation that you participate in that has an uplifting effect on your faith generally and faith toward Him.

"Now the Lord is the Spirit, and where the Spirit of the Lord is, there is freedom. We all, with unveiled faces, are looking as in a mirror at the glory of the Lord and are being transformed into the same image from glory to glory, this is from the Lord who is the Spirit. (2 Corinthians 3:17-18) Holman Christian Standard Bible)

You develop an intimate relationship with God by spending time before Him in devotion and in fellowship with Him by His Word, by His Spirit, waiting on Him in Praise and Worship. This interaction with the Almighty God by His Holy Spirt facilitates your meditation and revelation knowledge which in turn birth faith inside you. This is indeed a very powerful faith booster, because there is a level of revelation that only the Spirit of God can impart to your spirit. (1Cor 2:9).

Meditation in God's Word empowers you to be able to do the Word of God. Meditation on faith opens you up to the mystery of faith as the Author of the Word Himself explains to you directly from the Bible.

This quest for God and His Presence yields a bountiful harvest of spiritual power, as His Presence rubs off on you and you become a carrier of His power and anointing. His presence imparts to you the spirit of faith, which you cannot get any other way, except by impartation from the Word and the Holy Spirit. Fellowshipping with Him is like receiving double impartation.

As you learn to fellowship with God, you develop a sensitive spirit, to hear Him, speak to you. He is the Author and the Finisher or Developer of your faith. When He leads you in faith, He will provide the resources to manifest and fulfil His promises.

Praying In the Spirit Boosts Faith

Praying in tongues is another dimension communication with God, in the language of the Holy Spirit. The new bornagain believer has the spirit of God within him, otherwise, he cannot belong to God.

"But you are not in the flesh but in the Spirit, if indeed the Spirit of God dwells in you. Now if anyone does not have the Spirit of Christ, he is not His." (Romans 8:9)

"And because you are sons, God has sent forth the Spirit of His Son into your hearts, crying out, "Abba, Father!" (Galatians 4:6)

Although a new born-again believer has the Holy Spirt in him, his mind is not renewed and certainly does not have the fullness of the spirit, neither is he or she baptised in the Holy Ghost according to Acts 2:1-4 or Acts 19:1-8. Baptism in the Holy Ghost should normally be evidenced by speaking in unknown tongue.

According to the Bible, when you speak in an unknown tongue, your speaking is directed to God, unless you are in a gathering, when the interpretation of the tongue, by the manifestation of the Holy Spirit make completes the purpose of the tongue. When you speak in tongues, you speak divine mysteries and you also edify yourself or build up yourself spiritually.

"For he who speaks in a tongue does not speak to men but to God, for no one understands him; however, in the spirit he speaks mysteries. He who speaks in a tongue edifies himself, but he who prophesies edifies the church" (1 Corinthians 14:2, 4)

This factor of building up spiritual strength is the reason for Paul encouraging the believers to pray in the spirit – in tongues.

"For if I pray in a tongue, my spirit prays, but my understanding is unfruitful. What is the conclusion then? I

will pray with the spirit, and I will also pray with the understanding. I will sing with the spirit, and I will also sing with the understanding." (1 Corinthians 14:14-15)

This praying in tongue is the praying in the Holy Spirit tongue that Jude refers to as below:

"But you, beloved, building yourselves up on your most holy faith, praying in the Holy Spirit, keep yourselves in the love of God…" (Jude 1:21-22)

According to this scripture, praying in the spirit builds us up in our most holy faith – generally and specifically. As you pray in the spirit, you train yourself in spiritual things.

CHAPTER 9

FROM FAITH TO MANIFESTATION

I have decided to include about three of the messages or the write up for our weekly newsletter in this last chapter, to encourage you to continue to stand in faith. I also feel it is necessary to include this chapter, as a balance, because sometimes, when you get a revelation of the truth, and you try to share this revelation, it can appear lopsided and out of touch with reality. That is why the Word and the Holy Spirit are sometimes referred to as Wine; because they can be intoxicating, as the title of this book has been to me.

Jesus said that, *"in the world you shall have tribulation, but brace up, be cheerful because I have overcome the world."* (John 16:33)

We overcome by the blood of the lamb and the word of our testimony. So difficulties are common to man. Everyone experiences this. While it is true though, the essence of this book is that, you must not allow any difficulty to waylay you, neither must you allow it to overcome or derail your destiny. In this last chapter, I share how to stand, in victory, not in fear or anxiety – not with the mind-set of a victim. It is presented in note format.

Stand In Victory

Do not live life with a defeated attitude. Stand your ground and bring every issue under the dominion (control, supremacy or authority) of faith. Faith is the victory that overcomes the world. Jesus said 'In the world, Christians will have troubles, but be of good cheer' because the victory of Jesus belongs to you. Whether it is health, family, relationship or financial issues, we can walk through every challenge victoriously by faith.

While it is understandable that we sometimes feel discouraged, upset, overwhelmed or feel hopeless when trouble comes, God has designed for us and expects us to be courageous, and to "Deal With It! Today! Take a Position of Victory TODAY. Let's look at a few active steps you can take towards getting out of any problem you may be in. Although manifestation may not be instant, the victory can be instant, by faith. You can by faith receive your victory today and start seeing yourself with the answer. I trust that God will imprint the revelation of these steps into your life.

Steps to Victory over Any Problem

1. Let the Word Be Your Guide - not your instinct, not your spouse, not your government, not your bank account, not the society. Let the Word of God be the final authority in that problem or situation. Find some scriptures that promises you the answer. See Joshua 1:8.

2. **Fight the Good fight of Faith** - contend for your faith in God - Believe the Word in Your Heart, Meditate on it until there is no doubt, that you have your victory and declare with your mouth. Talk your Way Out of This Problem! See 1 John 5:4, 5

3. **Pray in the Spirit** - Speak in tongues, praying mysteries to the Father, about your situation. Do Spiritual Warfare: Some problems, not all - have spiritual origin(s). Walk in Discernment. Jehovah Nissi is your God - He is the Lord God Your Victory. Position yourself in battle. Be armed. See Ephesians 6:10-18

4. **Let God Lead you, and Be Obedient to Divine Instructions** - There is always a Divine Strategy for Victory over every trouble. Sometimes it does, but most times it doesn't make sense what God will ask you to do.

This is your test of Faith and trust in Him. Trust is not faith, but it is rested hope, once you are sure you are walking by faith. God will see you through. See Isaiah 42:6, Isaiah 48:17-19, Isaiah 40:1-3

5. **Speak to your Mentor and/or Counsellor or Pastor or Advocate.** Proverbs 11:14 "Where *there is* no counsel, the people fall; But in the multitude of counsellors *there is* safety."

You do not know everything there is to know, otherwise, this will not be a "problem". You have not done everything there is to do, otherwise, you will not be suffering. Speak to someone, and allow them to talk through Word-based, Spirit-led solutions, and then, let the Spirit of God, speak peace to you, regarding the most applicable option to follow, or steps to take.

6. Be still - even when the initial outcome looks unfavourable. Lemonade is made out of Lemon juice! Psalm 46:10. *"Be still, and know that I am God; I will be exalted among the nations, I will be exalted in the earth!"* There is no point worrying about the situation. When you worry or are afraid, the power of God cannot flow on your behalf, as you have learnt in this book. RELAX

7. Learn the Way of Praise - Casting Your Cares and Concerns on the Lord. By praise you establish your Dominion over the circumstances that are contrary to your expectation. By faith, you chase the devil out of your affairs, because God dwells inside your praise. See Acts 16:25-29, Chronicles 20:1-30. Praise is a powerful instrument of War.

Faith is a powerful step to allow God to fight your battle. Go ahead and break into dancing. You will see the mighty hand of God.

"But you are holy, Enthroned in the praises of Israel. "Our fathers trusted in you; they trusted, and you delivered them. They cried to you, and were delivered; they trusted in you,

and were not ashamed." (Psalms 22:3-5). You will not be ashamed in Jesus Name.

8. Take Courage. Be Fearless. The Storm will Soon Be Over – See Mark 4:35-40. Deuteronomy 31:6 Apply these steps to whatever you are going through right now, and may God give you understanding. Shalom

9. Be Conscious of Your Royalty - I perceive the Spirit of the Lord saying. Step Up, to the Pressure! Step up to the Pressure! Pressure Comes and Pressure Goes. For most times, it a very temporary phase or moment of our day and it quickly vanishes.

However, some pressures linger. They may be like hard nut, so difficult to crack. But God is the God of your Breakthroughs. No matter what the pressure may be, temporary or lingering, it's time for you to step up to the pressure. Give it what it takes.

Look at it right in the eye and say. I am bigger than you! For you, defeat is not an option, you must never consider or dwell on possible defeat. Victory should be on your mind. Triumph must be your goal, not failure.

But remember - There is always something next you have to do, in order to get you out. Usually, the starting point, is the point of faith. Believing again, that it is possible and that you are an overcomer and that you WILL - not may. You WILL get through this. Your God is Able and is ready to Help You.

"With God's power working in us, God can do much, much, more than anything we can ask or imagine." (Ephesians 3:20, NCV)

"But now thus saith the LORD that created thee? Fear not: for I have redeemed thee, I have called thee by thy name; thou art mine. - When thou passest through the waters, I will be with thee; and through the rivers, they shall not overflow thee: when thou walkest through the fire, thou shalt not be burned; neither shall the flame kindle upon thee." (Isaiah 43:1-2)

Be reassured in the faithfulness of God. There is no temptation that has come upon you, that is not common to man. God will make a way of escape for you, by providing the strength and the strategy to get you out. Praise God!

SHALOM! SHALOM! SHALOM!

NOTES

NOTES

NOTES

NOTES

NOTES

NOTES

ABOUT THE AUTHOR

Pastor Joe Daniels is the founder of Faith Heritage Ministries and visionary under-Shepherd of FHICC. He is a talented, creative and astute charismatic leader, an insightful possibility thinker and entrepreneur. He is a practising medical doctor, who has reached the top of his profession, as a consultant gynaecologist and is at the forefront of innovative medical concepts.

Pastor Daniels shares a passion for raising champions who are empowered and transformed in their thinking by the principles of the Word. He is married to Eunice and together, they are raising Godly family.

www.ingramcontent.com/pod-product-compliance
Lightning Source LLC
Chambersburg PA
CBHW071502040426
42444CB00008B/1464